Andrea Grace's Gentle Sleep Solutions

Andrea Grace's Gentle Sleep Solutions

ANDREA GRACE

First published in the UK in 2010 by Hodder & Stoughton
This newly revised edition published by Sheldon Press in 2022
An imprint of Hodder & Stoughton
An Hachette UK company

1

This book is for information or educational purposes only and is not
intended to act as a substitute for medical advice or treatment. Any
person with a condition requiring medical attention should consult a
qualified medical practitioner or suitable therapist.

British Library Cataloguing-in-Publication Data

A catalogue record for this book is available from the British Library.

Trade Paperback ISBN 978 1 399 80353 3
eBook ISBN 978 1 399 80352 6

Typeset by KnowledgeWorks Global Ltd.

Printed and bound in Great Britain by Clays Ltd, Elcograf S.p.A.

John Murray Press policy is to use papers that are natural, renewable and
recyclable products and made from wood grown in sustainable forests.
The logging and manufacturing processes are expected to conform to the
environmental regulations of the country of origin.

Sheldon Press
Hodder & Stoughton
Carmelite House
50 Victoria Embankment
London EC4Y 0DZ

www.sheldonpress.co.uk

Contents

Meet the author

Welcome to *Andrea Grace's Gentle Sleep Solutions*!

In *Andrea Grace's Gentle Sleep Solutions*, I want to give you the information that you need to address your baby's sleep problems in your own way. I believe that, as a parent, you know your child best. Sometimes, however, we all need a little help and this is especially true when it comes to handling our babies' sleep issues. When is it safe to drop night feeds? Is it cruel or even necessary to leave a baby to cry it out at night? How much daytime sleep should a baby have? What if my child is ill or has special needs? In this book, I address these questions and many more. What you will not find are detailed schedules telling you exactly what time to put your baby down for bedtime or nap time and when to wake her up again. Instead you will find the information you need in order to recognize your own baby's sleep needs. You will also find a range of safe and effective solutions. Out of these, I am sure that you will find one which you feel comfortable with. Once you have chosen your sleep training method, I will guide you through designing your own sleep plan and will support you as you implement it.

My interest in children's sleep arose from personal experience, when the eldest of my four children was a baby – and a truly terrible sleeper. Even though I was a qualified health visitor, I found that there was very little help available. Several years on, after lots of research and experience with many babies and families, I know that there are many different reasons for babies' sleep problems and certainly more than one solution. My intention is that by reading this book you will overcome your baby's sleep difficulty without compromising your own parenting style.

Preface

It is perfectly normal for babies to wake in the night. Certainly for the first few weeks, and sometimes months, they need your help to go back to sleep, whether it is to have a feed or sometimes just a cuddle. It takes time for them to develop and recognize the environmental factors that help to set their body clocks. For this reason, lack of sleep is a fact of life for all parents of new babies in the early days.

At around the third month, if not before, some babies start to sleep through the night, perhaps waking for just one night feed. For many, however, frequent night waking will continue or even increase long after this, into toddlerhood and sometimes into childhood. You might have noticed that your baby's sleep was fine in the early weeks but then deteriorated at around four to six months. This is a critical age, when babies' development leads them to a mature pattern of 90-minute sleep cycles and more definite sleep/wake phases. It is also the time of teething, and by six months many are moving to their own bedrooms, being introduced to solid food, certainly becoming more conscious of what is going on around them and learning fast! There are other times too, often during a developmental leap, or after an illness or a holiday, when your baby suddenly loses the ability to sleep well. When they don't sleep, it affects their mood and well-being, and it can also leave you feeling exhausted, helpless and worried.

About a quarter of all babies and children have a sleep problem at some point. You are not alone, and the really great news is that you *can* help your baby to overcome their sleep problem, using your natural ability and the guidance laid out in this book.

For starters, there are some 'golden rules' that you can follow, which will set you on the right path to help your baby to sleep well. These are:

- **Timing.** Teach your baby how to sleep when they are naturally most able to do so. For babies of over three months old, this is usually in the early evening. Leave a reasonable length of time before your baby has woken up from the last daytime nap before getting them ready for bed. How much time will depend on their age. Simply over-napping or sleeping very late in the afternoon can cause many infant sleep problems. With a younger baby, you need to make sure that they not overtired. In Chapter Two, you will find advice about 'awake windows' and naps.

- **Sleep cues.** Introduce a very consistent bedtime routine. A familiar series of steps leading up to bedtime will help a baby to feel both sleepy and safe. The routine should include a 'wind-down time', a nice warm bath, some repeated songs and phrases and lots of loving contact with you.

- **Bedtime book *after* the milk.** After the first weeks, try to avoid your baby falling asleep during the pre-bedtime milk feed. A good idea is to introduce a little picture book to look at together *after* the feed and before going to bed. If your baby can only settle while drinking milk, you may find that you have to give lots of nutritionally unnecessary feeds each time they stir during the light phase of a sleep cycle.

- **Love the cot!** It's good to put your baby into the cot while they are fully awake, as it can be alarming for them to wake later and find that they are no longer in your arms. Don't feel that you have to leave them alone if they cry. You can sit reassuringly beside them and pick them up for a cuddle if they need it. If your baby wakes in night, respond lovingly, but try to avoid bringing them into your bed, as if this happens a lot, it could make them think of their cot as just a temporary 'waiting area'.

- **Remember the sleep cycles.** It is normal for babies to wake several times during the night. Babies who are able to resettle themselves generally go to sleep independently at the beginning of the night, and are not expecting any night-time rituals, such as coming into your bed or having night feeds once they've outgrown the need for them.

If any of the above 'golden rules' are not happening for you and your baby, you might just have established what could be causing the problem, and if so, you are already on your way to improving your baby's (and your own) sleep.

If you treat the *cause* of your baby's sleep behaviour and not just the behaviour itself, you are much more likely to have a successful outcome. Not only this, but the learning process will usually be quicker and involve less crying.

Once you have got to the bottom of why your baby is waking a lot in the night, and made some changes to the way that you respond to the waking, you ultimately need to help them learn how to settle independently at the beginning of the night and to join their sleep cycles.

For this, choosing the sleep training method which sits best with you is important. There are various names given for different types of sleep training methods but basically, there are just two of them:

1. gradual withdrawal
2. controlled crying.

1. **Gradual withdrawal** is the gentlest technique, and it is perfect if you don't want to leave your baby alone to cry. It is good for younger babies, for babies who get very upset when you're not close by, and for those who have special health-care needs. It can sometimes take a long time before good sleep habits are established, but it will usually work

very well provided that you are clear about your goals and follow the method to its conclusion.

2. **Controlled crying** is a quicker method, that many babies and parents find tough at the time, but as it can take just one to three nights, it is soon over and done with. It is most suited to healthy babies over six months old, and parents who are either a bit more robust in their parenting style or at the end of their tether and need a speedy result. It is considered safe to do, provided that you are consistent and have well thought out sleep plan.

Although tackling a baby's sleep problem may be difficult to do at the time, it is well worth it, as sleep has huge health benefits. Babies who sleep well at night tend to be more settled and content in the day.

When *you* sleep well, you will be happier and healthier and naturally, your baby will benefit too.

Introduction

This book will teach you how to:

- understand the science of your baby's sleep
- recognize the nature of your child's sleep problem
- realize that you are not alone in having a sleepless baby
- get motivated for change
- choose the right solution for your baby and yourself
- design and implement your own tailor-made sleep plan – after all, you know your child better than anyone else.

The experience of parenting can be absolutely wonderful. The truth is that for many of us, it can also be exhausting and unnerving. This is especially the case if your child is awake and crying for much of the night.

If you have picked up this book, there is a good chance that you are one of literally thousands of parents with a baby who has a sleep problem. You may well be feeling tired and confused and be losing your confidence. Of course, you love your baby very much and you expected being a parent to be tiring, but this unrelenting exhaustion is more than you ever anticipated.

Well, here is some very good news for you: no matter how severe your baby's sleep problem is, how fragile she may be in terms of her needs or how low your tolerance for seeing her upset is, there is always something that you can do to improve her sleep.

If your baby is not sleeping there is a reason why not, and in this book you will find the information that you need to identify what is preventing your child from enjoying peaceful nights. More importantly, you will learn how to introduce gentle changes that will make all the difference to her sleep.

This book recognizes that each baby is an individual and that no single sleep solution is suitable for all. Once you have realized why your baby is sleeping badly, you will be able to choose from a range of solutions designed to suit both her needs and those of your family.

Not all babies and families fit into the same mould, thank goodness, and in recognizing this, you will find sections on babies with special needs, specific medical problems and particular family circumstances.

Did you know?

Even if your baby is fragile, because of a medical condition or other disability, there is a great deal that you can do to improve her potential for sleep.

In the following chapters you will discover something about the nature and value of babies' sleep. You will find practical advice on how much sleep your baby needs, how to establish a perfect bedtime routine, when and how to drop night feeds and what to do when things go wrong. You will find out what your baby needs in order to sleep well, safely and happily.

Once you have read the chapter on the nature of sleep, you should use the book as a manual, referring to the clearly laid-out chapters that address the needs of babies who are similar to your own.

There are lots of real-life case studies which it is hoped will strike a familiar chord with you. Although no two sleep problems are the same, just as no two babies are the same, many problematic sleepers share strikingly similar stories. It is hoped that you will find these helpful, not only in recognizing that you are not alone, but also in offering you some ideas about how to approach your own baby's sleeping problems. The case studies will inspire and motivate you to confidently make changes in the way that you handle your baby's sleep difficulties.

From Chapter 8 onwards you will find guidelines on how to identify your baby's sleep problem and you will then be guided through the planning, design, implementation and evaluation of a tailor-made sleep plan.

You will be surprised at what you can achieve and how quickly your sleep problem can be resolved. You will also see that teaching your child to sleep well can be a rewarding and positive experience.

Given that you are already up in the night attending to your baby, it makes sense to use that time wisely, in helping her learn to sleep happily all by herself.

As your child grows and learns life skills, such as communicating, getting mobile and enjoying her food, she will need your help, guidance and support. Exactly the same is true for learning sleep skills. Sleep is not only essential for good health and development; it is also one of life's simple pleasures. Taking the time to teach her how to enjoy sleep is a great investment and a wonderful gift from you to her.

When your baby is well rested, she will be more content, secure and better able to play and learn. Not only this, but when you get the rest that you so badly need, you will have the energy to maintain your other important relationships and interests. Most important of all, however, is that by successfully tackling your baby's sleep problem, your confidence as a parent will be restored and you will be able to truly enjoy your child's precious infancy.

Note

The male and female pronouns have been alternated in each chapter of this book. This is for convenience only and not because sleep problems at different ages are necessarily gender specific.

Many thanks to the Andrea Grace clients who have provided their family experiences for the case studies in this book.

1

Sleep: the facts and background

Given that this book is designed for parents of sleepless babies, it hardly needs to be stated that sleep is much more than just a functional state. Sleep is a wonderful, enjoyable process which, as well as helping us to function physically and mentally, is also a simple pleasure. Nothing can beat the feeling of slipping between the sheets of a cosy bed at the end of a hard day, or of staying in your warm bed for an extra hour on a weekend morning.

Babies can be helped to love their sleep, just as much as you do. During sleep, babies are able to grow, both mentally and physically. Their energy levels are restored and, as with adults, they are more likely to be cheerful and reasonable during the day as a result.

To my knowledge, no clinical trials involving deliberate sleep restriction have been done on babies to assess the effects of sleep deprivation, for obvious ethical reasons. It makes sense, however, to assume that babies are likely to suffer the effects of sleep deprivation, to some extent at least, in the same way that adults do.

Research into adult sleeplessness shows that sleep is vital for maintaining a healthy mind and body. Adults who are sleep-deprived run the risk of developing depression, poor concentration and a greater tendency to sustain injury through accidents. We are also beginning to understand that, when we are sleep-deprived, we are more susceptible to infection.

Despite this, we need to remember that babies, on the whole, are amazingly robust. Even those with poor night-time sleep seem to cope very well during the daylight hours.

Joshua has always been a gorgeous and cheery baby during the day. This was the case even when his night-time sleep was bad. Our friends, family and even our health visitor just couldn't believe it when we told them how difficult he was during the night. It wasn't easy to get the support that we needed to manage his sleep, because he was feeding well and looked so happy and healthy. I think people thought we were exaggerating. Now that he is sleeping well at night, we are able to get the sleep that we need, too. This means that we can fully enjoy our days with him.

Research from Cambridge University has shown that one very interesting difference between adults and children who are very tired is seen in their daytime behaviour. When adults are exhausted, we are likely to move and think more slowly, yawn a lot and feel very sleepy. In contrast, however, babies and young children become more active during the day when they are tired.

This overactivity is often accompanied by irritability and crying. Doesn't that sound familiar? This is typical 'overtired' behaviour, and it can have a negative impact on your baby's ability to settle to sleep, both for daytime naps and during the night.

Insight
Babies who are sleep-deprived during the night can become overactive during the day.

The nature of your baby's sleep

One of the most important things for us to understand when we come to assess our baby's sleep problem is that *it is perfectly normal for babies to wake up in the night*. Even those model babies who are 'good sleepers' will wake up several times during the night. What distinguishes good sleepers from those who have a sleep problem is the ability to resettle without help from their parents when they stir or wake up during the night.

Top tips

- If you want to increase the likelihood of your baby sleeping through the night, you need to encourage him to be aware that he is in his cot when he falls asleep at the beginning of the night.
- Babies who are placed into their cots only when they have gone to sleep are understandably confused or even alarmed when they stir in the night and find themselves in a different place.

When a baby goes to sleep at the beginning of the night, he does not embark on several hours of continuous deep unconsciousness. In many ways, sleep is still a rather mysterious process, but what we do know is that it comprises many different stages and cycles. These stages are made up of different types of sleep, which occur in cyclical patterns during the night, interspersed with brief arousals – in other words, waking up. The two main types of sleep are *rapid-eye-movement sleep*, or REM sleep, and *non-rapid-eye-movement sleep*, or NREM sleep.

REM and NREM sleep

These two terms define the main stages of sleep. You may have heard of them, but what exactly do they mean?

REM sleep is often referred to as 'active sleep' in babies. In adults, it forms the minority of our sleep time, at just 20 to 25 per cent of the total night's sleep. During this kind of sleep, muscle tone is almost absent and the body's ability to regulate its own temperature is temporarily suspended; paradoxically, the brain's activity is at its highest level. During REM sleep, dreaming is most likely to occur – in fact, REM sleep is sometimes called 'dream sleep'.

NREM or 'quiet' sleep occurs in four varying stages and in adults takes up the majority of the total night's sleep, averaging 75 to 80 per cent. This kind of sleep is very deep and restorative. During NREM sleep, your body will be calm and still.

REM sleep in babies

In newborn, full-term babies, REM sleep accounts for at least half of the total sleep period, and in premature babies, this 'active sleep' can account for around 80 per cent of all sleep. It is during this type of sleep that memory consolidation happens. Memory, of course, is very important for learning. The reason for this large amount of REM sleep in the early weeks is that it is important for the development of a baby's brain. You can tell when your baby is in REM sleep as his eyes will move rapidly under his eyelids. You may also notice some twitching of his body and even smiling. We know that the twitches in a new baby's sleep send sensory signals to the brain and these signals help to develop sensory and motor systems. During this kind of sleep, your baby is not able to maintain his body temperature by sweating or shivering. Because of this, you need to pay careful attention to helping him keep his body temperature just right. We will look at this more closely in the section on safe sleeping in Chapter 2.

NREM sleep in babies

During NREM sleep, your baby is less likely to be woken up by noise or movement. You may notice that his eye movements are slow and sweeping below his eyelids. Throughout his early weeks, he will begin to gradually increase the period of his NREM sleep, although it will take around six months of brain development before he moves into a mature pattern of NREM/REM sleep cycles and you are able to predict when his deep sleep is likely to occur. During NREM sleep, high levels of growth hormone is released – important of course, for your baby's growth and weight gain.

REM sleep
Looking at my baby, what do I see?

- His eyes are moving rapidly under his delicate eyelids.
- Although he is asleep, he is smiling occasionally.
- His breathing is fast and irregular.
- His little body twitches and jerks from time to time.

Why is he doing this?

- Even though he is sleeping, his brain is very active.
- He may be dreaming.
- This kind of 'active sleep' is normal, especially in tiny babies.

What should I do?

- Make sure that he is cosy, but not overheated, as he can't maintain his body temperature very well during REM sleep.
- Don't pick him up or wake him. He may look a little unsettled, but this special kind of sleep is important for his brain development.

NREM sleep
Looking at my baby, what do I see?

- His eyes may be moving in slow, sweeping motions beneath his eyelids.
- His body is calm and still.
- The expression on his face is peaceful.
- His breathing is slow and regular.
- He is undisturbed by moderate background noises.

Why is he doing this?

- He is in 'quiet sleep', which is the deepest kind.
- His body is both resting and growing.

What should I do?

- Leave him to sleep peacefully, but be aware that after this deep sleep phase, a period of more active sleep will follow.

The sleep cycles

The term 'sleep cycle' describes the transition from NREM sleep to REM sleep, followed by a brief 'wake up'. After the waking, a new sleep cycle begins again. These sleep cycles are repeated throughout the night.

Unlike older babies, new babies experience a phase of REM sleep at the beginning of the night, instead of the more usual NREM sleep. You will see, however, that, when your baby has matured a little, this initial REM sleep phase is replaced by NREM sleep. This usually occurs at around the age of three months. You may indeed have noticed that your baby settles well into peaceful sleep at the start of the night, only to wake up confused and upset half an hour or so later. The reason for this is very likely to be that he is in transition from NREM sleep to a period of REM sleep and does not yet have the skills to resettle by himself.

> When Emily got to four months old, she started to settle really well at bedtime with no crying or fuss. We noticed, though, that about half an hour later she would wake up and cry. Every night we had to go and resettle her, and although this only took a few moments, it was disruptive and it meant that we could never leave her with a babysitter. In the end, we started to cut down on the amount of patting we used to get her back off to sleep, and gradually she learned how to resettle herself. Although we still hear her call out occasionally at this time, we rarely now have to go to her.

In new babies, the usual length of a sleep cycle is around 50 minutes, but gradually extends to 90 minutes from the age of six months into adulthood. As a parent, you may be only too aware that, as the night progresses, your baby is more likely to become more restless and wakeful as dawn approaches. Typically, between three and six months, babies start to sleep in a relatively peaceful block at the beginning of the night, despite periods of REM sleep, but from the early hours onwards, sleep becomes much lighter and more fragile overall.

Top tips

- Early waking is normal in babies. You will find it easier to cope with if you are able to accept it and adjust your lifestyle to fit in with it.
- If at all possible, arrange with your partner to have one precious 'lie-in' each, perhaps on a weekend morning. You will both feel better for it.
- Go to bed early. Even if you are usually a 'night owl', your body will adjust to its new timetable.
- Avoid drinking alcohol. As well as being unsafe, being 'under the influence' will make getting up in the early morning ten times worse.

The circadian clock

Human beings and animals have an internal clock that tells us the difference between night and day. Newborn babies do not automatically recognize bedtime, and their sleeping time is divided more or less equally between night and day. As your baby matures, however, he will start to produce sleep/wake hormones which helps him to sleep more at night and less during the day. This is called the circadian rhythm.

The circadian clock (or biological clock) is situated in an area of the brain known as the hypothalamus. So that it can work well, it needs external clues such as differing levels of light and darkness. It also responds to conditions within your baby's own body, such as temperature, hunger and hormone levels. In the early weeks, babies do not produce their own sleep hormone (melatonin) and therefore their circadian rhythm is strongly connected to their mum. But as they grow, and experience daytime brightness and night-time darkness, they start to produce their own levels of melatonin. This is usually happens by the third month, if not before.

Melatonin versus cortisol

Melatonin, which is produced in the pineal gland, is the hormone that promotes sleep. Cortisol, which is produced in the cortex of the adrenal gland, is the hormone associated with wakefulness. Levels of this 'awake hormone' are at their highest first thing in the morning. You may have noticed that your baby is at her most smiley and communicative when she first wakes up. Under the influence of the circadian clock, these two hormones work in harmony to regulate your baby's sleep and wake patterns. Cortisol is also known as a stress hormone. Sometimes, a baby will produce too much cortisol, and this will cause her to be wakeful even when she is tired. The most common reason for babies having high cortisol levels are:

- being overtired.
- being left alone to cry
- too much noise
- too much light exposure – especially to screens.

Sleep pressure and awake windows

Baby sleep, as we have seen, is influenced by hormone levels; but there is also another really important factor that affects the way that your baby sleeps. This is called *homeostasis*, and it is the way the body regulates and maintains its health and balance. Things like body temperature and hunger levels are controlled by the body's homeostasis – and so is sleep. To feel sleepy, we all need to experience a rise in *sleep pressure*. Sleep pressure builds up when we are awake, and when we're talking about babies' sleep, we call these periods of wakefulness *awake windows*. The younger the baby and the quicker the build-up of sleep pressure, the smaller the awake windows. As babies get older, they naturally space out the naps, extend the awake windows and also take less daytime sleep overall.

A one-week-old baby will need to sleep about every hour or less, whereas a toddler of 18 months, can have an awake window of four to five hours before needing sleep. As we know, when babies are overtired, they can feel stressed and this causes a rise in cortisol and sometimes adrenaline – both of which fight against the sleep hormones. With this in mind, it is good to keep an eye on the awake windows, give your baby the opportunity to sleep when he needs to, and recognize that, in the early days, he will need to sleep a lot.

Top tips

- Helping your baby to develop a consistent routine for both daytime and night-time will help his body recognize the difference between night and day. You should also try to incorporate some other day/night cues into his environment, such as altering the levels of light and noise so that they are appropriate for the time of day.
- Milk contains an amino acid called tryptophan, which the body uses to make melatonin. That is why a milky drink is a well-known and effective sleep aid. Breastfed babies benefit from the fact that late in the day and at night time, levels of tryptophan in breast milk are raised – which is good news. However, because breast milk can be more quickly digested than formula milk, breastfed babies tend to continue with night feeds for longer than formula fed babies do.
- Exposure to daylight, especially in the morning, will speed along the process of his own sleep hormone production, as will having dark conditions for sleep time.

Insight

One of the reasons that being woken in the night as a parent is so debilitating is that there is every chance that you are being pulled out of the deeply restorative NREM sleep. Your baby, however, is more likely to wake during or just after the active REM sleep. This explains why, the following day, he is still smiling and you are on your knees.

How much sleep do babies need?

Nought to six weeks

In these early, precious but exhausting weeks, sleep is very closely involved with feeding. Your new baby will tend to live life in a milky, dozy state. It is quite usual to feed him every two to three hours. As we have already seen, few very young babies really settle into a period of quiet, deep sleep.

Babies of this age tend to sleep for 15–18 hours in a 24-hour period.

For the first two or three months, many babies prefer to sleep in your arms or laid on your chest. This period is sometimes called the 'fourth trimester'.

Six to 16 weeks

By this stage many babies are beginning to sleep for longer periods and to feed less often. It is usual for a baby of about eight weeks to sleep for up to six hours at night without waking for a feed, although many babies have managed to do this earlier and some will be a little later.

A baby's total sleep requirement may have dropped slightly, to between 14 and 16 hours per day, but sleep will be becoming deeper and lasting for longer periods.

Four to six months

At this lovely age, your baby is becoming much more active. By six months he might have started to enjoy solid food. He will probably still be waking for night feeds, but these may now be reducing, as he gets bigger. Some, but not all, babies will drop some or all of their night feeds around this age (see Chapter 4).

By now it is possible that he will be sleeping for between six and ten hours a night, with two to four daytime naps. This should total about 14–15 hours. For some babies, however, sleep can get worse at this age. See Chapter 3 for advice about the 'four-month sleep regression'.

Six to 12 months

By now your baby is likely to be very active indeed. The 'average' baby sits up independently at six months, crawls at nine months and begins to toddle at one year old. These stages of your child's development are tremendously rewarding, but can be exhausting, too. Sometimes, when a baby learns a new skill, they can experience a brief period of sleep regression. This can be frustrating because both you and your baby need sleep more than ever before.

Babies of this age tend to naturally drop their night feeds, and as they reach 12 months, they do not normally need them for nutritional reasons. In fact, sometimes if a baby has a small appetite in the day or is very fussy with solids, it can be because they are feeding a lot at night.

Your baby requires 13–14 hours sleep in a 24-hour period. This is usually made up of a night-time sleep of 10–12 hours, plus a morning and an afternoon nap.

Twelve months to two years

In the second year of life, when your baby is growing at a tremendous rate and is likely to be racing around, his sleep requirement remains at around 12–14 hours in a 24-hour period. He may, however, drop one of his daytime naps and instead take just one long nap in the middle of the day.

Babies' average hours of sleep

Age	Hours of sleep
0–6 weeks (healthy full-term baby)	15–18 hours
6–16 weeks	14–16 hours
4–6 months	14–15 hours
6–12 months	13–14 hours
12–24 months	12–13 hours

Ten things to remember

1. It is normal and healthy for babies to wake at night.
2. New babies are asleep more than they are awake, and they experience lots of 'active' REM sleep.
3. They settle into a mature circadian rhythm at about three months old.
4. It is best to feed on demand for the first few weeks – especially if you are breastfeeding.
5. Exposure to daylight and darkness helps your baby's sleep hormone production.
6. Many babies start to sleep for six to ten hours at night at around four months, but a lot of them can start waking more often at this age.
7. A sleep problem can arise when an older baby is not able to put themselves back to sleep when they wake in the night.
8. The best time to 'teach' a baby how to fall asleep in the cot is at the start of the night, when her melatonin levels are high and cortisol levels are low.
9. Overtiredness and excess crying can cause raised cortisol levels and affect a baby's ability to relax and sleep well.
10. Having a calm, quiet atmosphere, with low lighting and no screen exposure at bedtime, will help a baby to sleep well.

2

What every baby needs for a good night's sleep

Introducing a good bedtime routine is the single most important thing that you can do to help your baby sleep well through the night. Unfortunately, for many of us, at the end of a busy and tiring day, we have few resources and even less energy to make the effort to create a lovely routine for our babies. However, once you realize just what a difference it will make, not just for your baby, but for you, too, you will find the motivation to put this into place.

The best bedtime routine provides *a familiar series of steps* leading up to bedtime and sleep. Each of these steps will in time become a mini-sleep trigger for your baby. Your child's bedtime routine can be as short and sweet or as long as you like, providing that it can be worked into your daily life and is implemented in a loving and consistent manner. When you come to plan your bedtime routine, you need to take into account your family's ethos, values and practical circumstances.

Getting the timing right

If a bedtime routine is to be really effective, it needs to conclude with your baby going off to sleep. For this reason, you need to pay attention to *timing*. There is no point going through the whole bedtime preparation process only to bring your baby back into the living room to play or watch a video. You need to begin your routine around half an hour or so before you know your child is ready to go to sleep.

> **Insight**
> You should only begin your bedtime routine when you know that your child is ready to sleep. The process of the routine is more important than the time at which it is carried out.

If you have been unable to prevent your baby from sleeping late in the afternoon, it makes sense to begin her bedtime routine later in the evening, rather than rigidly sticking to a set bedtime. This way, she will be nice and sleepy by the end of the routine and ready to go into her cot. Putting her to bed with lots of energy to spare is likely to result in her crying and calling for you, and can result in her developing negative associations with bedtime.

Sleep triggers

Any repeated action which is associated with falling asleep will very soon become a sleep trigger. This is why a consistent bedtime routine is so very important and so useful to you as a parent. Choose your sleep triggers carefully and try to make them simple and fun – after all, you will be using them every day.

> **Sleep triggers**
> - Warm bath
> - Familiar song or splashing game in the bath
> - Massage
> - Familiar spoken ritual or story book before putting your baby into the cot
> - Familiar parting ritual before leaving your baby to settle for the night

Bath time

Introducing a nightly bath early on in your baby's life will really help to promote good sleep for her. The action of taking a bath before bed provides a clear signal that daytime is now coming to an end and sleep time is on its way. This is particularly effective if you make sure that you have all you need to settle your baby for the night when you begin bath time, so you can avoid having to return to the living room. Research has shown that the cooling-down process that follows a warm bath helps to induce sleep, so all the more reason to have a nightly bath as part of your baby's routine.

Try to make bath time a lovely part of the day for both of you. Turn off the TV and put your phone away. This is a special time for you and your child and an ideal opportunity to handle her in a loving way. Having this close contact and attention from you will make her feel happy and content – just the way she should feel before settling for the night.

Don't worry if bath time is full of splashing and noisy fun. Your baby is simply expending her reserves of energy, and this is a good thing. The time for soft lighting and quiet voices is when you take her to her room.

In many families, it is the partner's job to bath the baby, perhaps when they come home from work. This is a lovely thing to do, as it helps to develop a loving bond between the other parent and baby. Once again, if your baby gets very wakeful and excited at the other parent's arrival, this need not be a problem. Provided that this is built into the consistent ritual of the bedtime routine, it will still act as a sleep trigger.

Parents of babies with eczema and other dry skin conditions are sometimes advised not to bath their babies daily. Of course, you need to accept expert advice, but most paediatricians and dermatologists nowadays would advise a daily warm (not too hot) bath in water to which a special moisturizer has been added. Do check with your doctor or health visitor if you are unsure, as it is a shame for children with dry skin to miss out on this lovely and soothing bath-time ritual.

If you prefer to bath your baby in the morning or do not have access to bathing facilities, you can introduce elements of the nightly bath-time routine, such as a naked kick around on the changing mat and a gentle splashing song into your wash and change routine.

Other sleep cues

Try to avoid the complicated use of mobiles, light shows, DVDs, music and so on during your bedtime routine. These things can be cumbersome and liable to break down. They can also, potentially, make life very difficult for you when you go away on holiday. The best sleep triggers are *portable*, and the most portable of all are those actions and words performed by you.

The wonderful thing about a good bedtime routine is that not only does it help a baby to feel sleepy, it also helps her to feel safe and content. Babies and children absolutely love ritual, routine and predictability. Try putting yourself in your baby's position: when you were little and dependent on others, routine helped you to feel safely contained and cared for.

A great routine

- Begin your routine shortly before you know your baby is ready for sleep.
- Take everything that you need for the night with you, to avoid having to come back into the living area.
- Follow a similar bedtime 'script' by using familiar phrases and actions at key points during the routine.
- Bath every night unless there are genuine reasons why you can't. Sing the same 'action' song in the bath each night.
- Go directly to your baby's sleep room after the bath.
- Change her into a clean nappy.
- Give her a milk feed.
- Read a story or sing a goodnight song.
- Place her into the cot, awake but sleepy, to settle for the night.

When Thea was newly born, I breastfed her on demand and didn't worry too much about establishing a bedtime routine. Her dad and I are both quite laid back and we didn't like the idea of our first baby having to fit in with some kind of strict regime. We were very happy to have her up with us most evenings, especially as she was growing well and was such a delight to be with. However, when she was six months old, I felt that Thea was becoming more and more unsettled and needed to have a little more structure. I think, too, that we needed to have more time together in the evenings as a couple.

We decided to try introducing a bedtime routine and to make it a loving family time. Her dad was responsible for bathing and changing her and I then fed her, read to her and put her in her cot. We found that, far from being restrictive, the whole routine thing opened up a new way of enjoying her. Thea loved having Daddy bath her and the special quiet time with me, too. We have found that, since introducing the routine, she sleeps much better and is generally much more settled.

I realize in retrospect that we could have started earlier on this, and that there were times in the evenings when she was unsettled and we were carrying her round with us – passing her between each other to try and comfort her, when she was, in reality, just overtired and needing some structure and her own space.

Later in this book you will learn how to teach your baby the skill of going to sleep without having you beside her. In preparation for this, you need to establish a good routine and to be aware if your child is falling asleep in a way that is likely to cause her to wake and cry for you during the night, when she goes through the light phase of a sleep cycle.

Unhelpful settling habits include:

- falling asleep over her milk feed
- being cuddled or rocked in your arms until she is asleep

- twiddling your hair or pinching your skin (more common than you might think)
- using her dummy (pacifier) to induce sleep – except in the early weeks if she has colic or reflux. (You might want to look at the later section covering this, as well as the one on dummy use.)

Safe sleeping for babies: how to reduce the risk of cot death

When undertaking sleep training of any kind, it goes without saying that the safety of your child is of paramount importance. Whether you are considering sleep training or not, you need to be sure that your child is safe at bedtime and during sleep.

Although relatively uncommon, cot death – medically known as sudden infant death syndrome (SIDS) – is every parent's worst fear. Fortunately, there are some simple steps that you are able to take in order to reduce the risk of this tragedy occurring. The following guide is based on information from The Lullaby Trust.

Positioning

The safest position for your baby to sleep in is on her back. She should also be placed with her feet at the foot of the cot, with the bedding tucked in and made up to come no higher than her shoulders. This is so that she can't wriggle down under her blankets. Do not position your baby's bed near to a radiator or heater of any kind. The cot should be kept away from direct sunlight, too.

It is recommended that babies sleep in a crib or cot in the same room as a parent until six months old. In the very early weeks, many parents have the cot close to the side of their bed for ease of feeding. Once your baby is not taking night feeds, you might want to place the cot at the foot of your bed, where she can't see you so easily. This way, if you are planning to move her to her own room later, she will have had a little 'stepping stone' towards sleeping alone.

Bedding

Duvets and pillows are not recommended for babies under one year. It is far safer to use a cotton sheet and light layers of cotton blankets. Electric blankets and hot water bottles should never be used.

It is fine to use a baby sleeping bag. They are great for keeping babies cosy, but they need to be cotton, lightweight and not have a hood. It is most important that the sleeping bag is the right size. If it is too big, your baby could potentially slip down into the bag; too small and it will be uncomfortable and restrictive.

The cot

Your baby's cot should be clear – with no toys, pillows, loose bedding or bumpers. Your baby needs to sleep on a firm, flat surface. Ideally, the mattress should be new. If yours was inherited from a family member or a friend, you need to make sure that it is clean, dry and free from cracks and tears. It should be firm, with no sagging and fit the cot snugly, with no gaps at the edges. Ventilated mattresses with holes are not recommended, as they are impossible to keep clean. Your baby should not sleep on a pillow, bean bag, sofa or waterbed.

The use of cot bumpers is considered to be dangerous by some, and The Lullaby Trust currently advises against them, but recommends that if a bumper is used, it should meet British Standards. If you decide to use a cot bumper, it is advisable to remove it once your baby is able to get on to her hands and knees, as she may potentially use it as a means to climb out of her cot.

Temperature

The recommended room temperature for a baby is 16–20°C (61–68°F). For many of us, this feels rather cool, but research has shown that it is a safe and comfortable temperature for a baby to sleep in. In ordinary circumstances, it is not recommended that central heating be left on overnight, unless it is controlled by a thermostat.

To see if your baby is too hot or too cold, you should feel her tummy or neck, but not her hands or feet, as they often feel quite cool.

Do check that your baby is not hot and sweaty during sleep.

Sleeping with you

The safest place for your baby to sleep is in her cot, on her back. For the first six months, it is best for her cot to be in a room with you. If there is not enough space, you should have her in the next nearest room, with the doors left open.

You should especially avoid having your baby sleep in bed with you if:

- either parent is a smoker (even if you don't smoke at home)
- either of you have been drinking alcohol or have taken drugs or medication which might cause drowsiness
- either of you is very tired
- your baby was premature or of low birth weight (less than 2.5 kg / 5.5 lb)
- your baby is under three months old.

If you do choose to have your baby sleep in bed with you, you need to be aware of the dangers of you rolling over and suffocating her, and of her falling out of the bed or getting trapped between the bed and the wall. Watch out for accidents, and make sure that her head is uncovered and not near the pillow and that her covers are light. Never sleep with her on a sofa or in an armchair., either at night or during the day.

Top tip

Before commencing any kind of sleep training that may involve leaving your child alone to cry, you should be quite confident that she is healthy and has no temperature and that her environment is safe.

Guidelines for reducing the risk of cot death

- Cut out smoking in pregnancy – this includes partners, too.
- Do not let anyone smoke in the same room as your baby.
- Place your baby on her back to sleep.
- Do not let your baby get too hot.
- Keep your baby's head uncovered – place her with her feet at the foot of the cot, to prevent wriggling down under the covers.
- If your baby is unwell, seek medical advice promptly.
- The safest place for your baby to sleep is in a cot in your room for the first six months.
- Do not share a bed with your baby, especially if:
  - you or your partner smoke – even if away from the home
  - either you or your partner have been drinking alcohol
  - you or your partner take medication or drugs that make you drowsy
  - you or your partner feel very tired
  - your baby was born prematurely or was small at birth
- Never sleep with a baby on a sofa or armchair.

Daytime naps

In recent years, there has been a swing back to the practice of offering babies structured feeds and a controlled regime of daytime naps, ideally taken in a cot. Parents often express concern that they are unable to achieve consistency with naps and that the need to care for older children means that they are often out of the home at nap times and therefore unable to settle the baby in her cot.

However, as long as she is given the opportunity to sleep during the day, whether it is in the cot, pram, sling or even in the car seat, she will still benefit from her naps.

Insight

Your baby does not have to be at home in her cot to enjoy the benefits of a daytime nap.

I already had two-year-old Pietro when Sofia arrived. I was worried that I wouldn't be able to give her the same structured nap regime that he had had when he was small, as we were constantly on the move between various activities. Even when we were at home, the house never seemed to be quiet.

Sofia has managed to fit her naps in when she is out in the pram, and it hasn't taken her long to settle into a pattern where her main nap of the day is now taken in her cot at the same time that Pietro has his.

In the end, I really don't think she has suffered from the lack of structure during the day. In fact, if anything, I think that she has benefited by learning to be more flexible about where she sleeps. She is far more easy-going now than her brother was at her age.

To establish a natural pattern of napping, it makes sense to watch for the signs that your baby is becoming tired and to follow her lead. This approach is more likely to be successful than imposing a prescribed sleeping schedule on her. You need, however, to avoid allowing her to become overtired, as this will make it difficult for her to settle.

It is better to be aware of your baby's usual awake windows and then encourage her to nap when she is relaxed and ready for sleep.

A rough guide to awake windows (or how often your baby will need to sleep)

Age	Awake windows
Newborn–2 weeks	Baby sleeps on and off for most of the time
2–8 weeks	1–1.5 hours
8–12 weeks	1.5–2 hours
3–6 months	2–3 hours
6–12 months:	2.5–4 hours
12–24 months	4–5 hours

Signs that your child is becoming tired include:

- glancing away from you/not holding eye contact/staring into the distance
- reddening around her eyes
- rubbing her eyes or eyebrows
- yawning
- becoming irritable
- crying.

The following techniques will help you settle your baby for a nap:

- About ten minutes before you think that she will be ready to sleep, take her to her room and have a calm 'wind-down' time, looking at books or having some gentle music.
- Have the room dark or a have a shade over the pram. Don't worry about day/night confusion. The important message is let her know that now it's time for sleep.
- If you're at home and putting her into her cot, use a mini bedtime routine with a nappy change, the same bedtime book, curtains closed, and so on, and then settle her in the same way as you do at night-time.
- Don't risk breaking her build-up of sleep pressure by rocking/cuddling her nearly to sleep and then putting her into the

cot. Put her down fully awake or fully asleep. 'Drowsy but awake' often doesn't work.

- If she wakes soon after going to sleep and still appears to be tired, then you can spend another 15 minutes or so trying to help her to resettle in the cot.
- If, after this time, she is showing no signs of going back to sleep, you can get her up and either let her extend the nap out in the pram/your arms/a sling or push on and bring the next nap or bedtime forward.
- You should avoid any aggressive 'cry it out' techniques which may not lead to her extending the nap and may set up a negative association with the cot.
- Equally, not having enough daytime sleep can cause your baby to become overtired and irritable at bedtime, leading to settling and sleeping problems.
- An overtired baby will often either refuse her feed or fall asleep over it, resulting in her being hungry later on.
- If your baby is taking erratic, inconsistent naps during the day, concentrate your efforts on establishing good sleep habits at night.
- Once your baby has learned good night-time sleep skills, she will be able to transfer them to her daytime naps too.

Averages for daytime naps

Age	Number of naps per day	Total sleep time
0–6 weeks	4–8	7.5–9 hours
6–8 weeks	4–6	approx. 6 hours
2–3 months	4–5	3.5–5 hours
4–6 months	3–4	approx. 3–4 hours
7–12 months	2	2–3.5 hours
13–24 months	1 nap*	1.5 hours

* Usually taken in the middle of the day; up to around 18 months, there may be a second, shorter nap taken either in the morning or later in the afternoon.

Does your child have a sleep problem?

We don't all bring up our children in the same way, and just as our approaches to such things as feeding, health care and our little ones' behaviour are varied, so are our attitudes and feelings about the way that our children sleep.

Some parents are strictly of the 'bath–milk–cot–leave alone to sleep' school, while at the other end of the scale are those who prefer feeding or cuddling their child to sleep and are fine about doing the same when they wake during the night. Many start their journey intending to be strict/soft and so on but end up changing course as they follow their baby's lead.

It's important to respect both parenting styles and understand that some parents need to be in control of what's happening with their child's sleep and to have them sleeping perfectly consistently and well both day and night in order to cope with the pressures of their working lives or for their own mental health.

Babies learn how to sleep through the night at different ages. For some this will be in the very early weeks, but for others it may take a year or more. There is no doubt, too, that some babies find sleep more easy or difficult than others. To establish whether or not your child has a sleep problem, ask yourself the following questions:

1. Is she happy and content when she is awake?
2. Does she wake up gradually and happily?
3. Does she fall asleep without too much crying?
4. Is she feeding well?
5. Is she growing well and putting on the right amount of weight?
6. If she is over three months, is she able to fall asleep without being physically attached to you?
7. Are you enjoying her infancy and being close to her?

If you have answered 'yes' to most of these, the chances are that, even if your child might not sleep right through the night, she is getting enough sleep. If you answered 'no', you need to ask yourself the next few questions:

1. Does she wake up more in the night than she used to do?
2. Is she cranky and irritable when she is awake?
3. Does she often fall asleep during her feeds or struggle to feed?
4. Are you concerned about her weight gain?
5. Does she sleep for very short bursts and wake up suddenly, distressed?
6. Are you finding being with her stressful and difficult?
7. Are you exhausted and struggling to cope?

If you answered mainly 'yes' to these questions, and you have ruled out that she might be unwell, your baby probably does have a sleep problem. Don't worry, though: there is always a solution, no matter how severe the problem is. Find the section in this book that best describes your baby's age and make your way there. Help is at hand.

Ten things to remember

1. Establishing a good bedtime routine is one of the best things you can do to help your baby sleep.
2. It is important that your baby is sufficiently tired but not overtired at bedtime. This might mean that the time you put them to bed may vary.
3. The repeated actions in a bedtime routine will act as a series of sleep triggers.
4. These actions/triggers should be highly portable and not depend on bulky or expensive equipment.
5. A bath close to bedtime will promote good sleep.
6. Always follow the guidelines from The Lullaby Trust to keep your baby safe.
7. Daytime naps are important but they do not have to be taken at home.
8. No matter how severe your baby's sleep problem is, there is always something you can do to improve things. And it's never too late.
9. Be realistic in your expectations of your child's sleep – it's normal for younger babies to wake in the night – and most babies do wake up early!
10. It is up to the parents to decide whether their child has a sleep problem. You know your baby best. If other people tell you that your baby has a sleep problem, but you feel that they are doing fine, you baby does not have a sleep problem.

3

Sleep advice for the first six months

Nought to six weeks

During these amazing first weeks, your first concern needs to be that your baby's feeding, whether it is with breast milk or formula, becomes established and is working well. It is important that you are confident that your baby is growing steadily. At this age, some babies can develop reflux, which may affect their sleeping. This is discussed in Chapter 7.

It is also very important that you spend lots of time holding and cuddling your baby. Remember that until very recently he was held securely in the warmth of his mother's womb. If constant holding is difficult for you, you might like to try using a well-fitting and supportive sling-type baby-carrier for some of the day. This way, you can keep your baby close to you while getting on with other jobs. Remember, however, that, as a new mother, it is important that you rest as much as you can during this time, so don't try and overdo things.

At night-time, if your baby seems to need constant holding, you might like to consider swaddling him. Swaddling has been an effective way of calming babies for centuries. It is a method of wrapping a baby to re-create the secure feeling of being held.

> ## Top tips: how to swaddle your baby
>
> 1 Spread out a pure cotton baby flat-sheet with the right-hand corner folded down slightly.
> 2 Lay your baby on the sheet face up, with his neck against the fold.

3 Pull the top left-hand corner across his body and tuck it behind his right arm, smoothly under his back.

4 Pull the bottom right corner up and across to under his chin.

5 Bring the bottom left corner diagonally over his right shoulder and tuck it in at the back.

6 Now check that the swaddling is firm but not too tight, and that your baby's face and head are uncovered.

If your baby is wearing a vest and sleepsuit, this is probably all the bedding he will need.

Swaddling is a lovely alternative to being held, although not all babies like it. For obvious reasons, it is especially unsuitable for babies who like to suck their thumb. It is really only suitable for babies in the early weeks, before they are able to roll over.

If you decide to introduce your baby to a swaddle, follow these golden rules:

- If you swaddle your baby as part of their usual sleep routine, it is best to do it for both night sleeps and day sleeps, too.
- The Lullaby Trust is neither for nor against swaddling, but a few years ago some research suggested that it is safest to introduce a swaddle in the earliest weeks, and not after three months.
- Use a light cotton material and make sure that the swaddling finishes at shoulder height. Your baby's head *must* be uncovered.
- Never place your baby to sleep on their front – *especially* when they are swaddled.
- Don't have your swaddled baby in bed with you.
- The swaddling should be used *instead* of other bedding, and not in addition to it – so no extra covers.
- Use cotton clothing under the swaddle and layer according to how warm/cool your baby is and also how warm/cool the

room is. Check your baby's temperature by feeling their back or chest (not hands and feet as young baby's extremities are naturally cool).

- Do not allow your baby to get too hot. The room temperature should be 61–68°F (16–20°C).
- You can make your own swaddle from a piece of cotton sheeting or you can buy pre-made swaddles.
- Sometime between four and six months, it is likely that your baby will learn how to roll over. When you can see that this is about to happen, you will need to get rid of the swaddle. They will need their arms free to roll both ways and to prevent them from getting stuck on their front.

In Chapter 1, we have seen that babies of nought to six weeks tend to sleep for around 15–18 hours in a 24-hour period. If you think that your baby isn't getting this much sleep, why not keep a simple sleep diary? This will give you a clearer picture of his sleep habits and will enable you to see if any pattern is beginning to emerge.

Remember, though, that at this age a baby's sleep tends to be quite light and yours may be sleeping during his feeds.

Try not to feel discouraged if your baby does not sleep through the night at this age. It might not feel like it, but most babies do not sleep through yet. Provided that you give him plenty of love, care and food and help him to feel safe and secure, you will be maximizing his potential for good sleep.

Remember that, if you are breastfeeding, it may take a little longer for night feeding to stop than if you are using formula. These night breast feeds are necessary, as it is during the night that mothers' levels of prolactin (the hormone responsible for milk production) are at their highest. In these early weeks, night feeding will ensure that you have enough milk to meet your baby's needs during the coming day.

Insight

'Cluster feeding' (giving several feeds in the early evening) a tired and fractious baby at the end of the day can be a good thing. Not only will it fill his tummy, but research has shown that, towards the end of the day, breast milk contains higher amounts of the sleep-promoting amino acid tryptophan.

Nought to six weeks: your baby's top sleep needs

- Enough milk – if you are breastfeeding, this means feeding on demand. For formula-fed babies, you need to offer him about 2½ oz (75 ml) milk per pound (0.45 kg) of his body weight in a 24-hour period.
- A warm, safe and cosy place to sleep.
- Frequent daytime naps to prevent overtiredness.
- Exposure to daylight, and a different and darker sleep environment at night, to encourage production of the light-dependent sleep hormone (melatonin).
- Having the lights kept low and as little noise as possible during the night. Do not change the baby's nappy unless it is very wet or is soiled. A thermos with warm water for cleaning him will save you crashing around in the bathroom in the middle of the night.
- The introduction of a familiar gentle song that your baby will come to associate with bedtime.

Six weeks to four months

At around six weeks, you will receive your baby's first smile. This wonderful moment often heralds the start of a period of more settled sleep, too. It often takes about six or eight weeks for breastfeeding to become fully established and for a baby to grow to be truly settled and contented. We have seen, too, in Chapter 1 how babies' sleep abilities are beginning to develop at around this age. Many parents will notice that their babies are sleeping for longer periods during the night. This is partly because they are bigger and more robust, even though they are still just milk-fed and will not move on to taking solid food until they are six months old.

Your baby's total sleep requirement may have dropped slightly, to between 14 and 16 hours per day, but his sleep will be deeper and last for longer periods.

To encourage good sleeping habits at this age, continue to meet your baby's first needs as outlined above, and in addition try to persuade him to sleep without feeding.

Six weeks to four months: your baby's top sleep needs

- Regular feeds: try to give larger, less frequent feeds.
- A very simple bedtime routine: if possible, set it to coincide with the time just before your baby usually sleeps for his longest period.
- The same comfortable, safe sleeping environment: you may need to move from Moses basket to cot.
- Encourage your baby to sleep without sucking: feed him until he is full and sleepy and then wind him well. Place him in his cot and settle him by patting or stroking if necessary.

Of course, for many babies this age can represent a difficult rather than a settled time. Common ailments such as colic, reflux, milk allergy and infantile eczema will have an adverse effect on the development of good sleep skills. Please see Chapter 7 for advice on how to manage your baby's sleep when faced with these special conditions.

Four to six months

By now, your baby is becoming more settled and his sleep patterns are more predictable. Daytimes may be getting easier, too, as your baby learns how to watch you and be entertained by what is going on around him. You need to provide him with a rich and varied environment to keep him stimulated. Rather than keep him in the same room all day, take him with you in his baby chair as you go from room to room. Chat to him as much as you can and give him lots of smiles. This will encourage him to develop his own lovely language. When he begins to make cooing and then babbling sounds, respond to him warmly and encourage him to carry on. If your baby uses a dummy, just keep it for sleep times. Putting a dummy into his mouth every time he makes a sound may impair the development of his speech.

When he is awake and at home, take advantage of the fact that he can now hold a toy and reach out to his baby gym by providing him with lots to look at, hold and touch. Also, change his position regularly, both to encourage his physical strength and motor development and to prevent him from becoming bored. Try laying him on his back and then on his tummy, as well as having him reclining in his baby chair. Many babies are beginning to sit up straight and unsupported at around six months, and this independence increases the scope for activities.

Try to make sure that you go outside at least once a day, so that he can experience some sunlight, although you will need to protect his delicate skin with shade and sun block if the weather is warm or the sun is strong. Unfortunately, all too often, parents are reluctant to go out during the day as they feel they have to stick to a schedule whereby their baby naps only in his cot. Don't worry if he falls asleep in his pram. A nap taken in the pram (or car or sling for that matter) is every bit as valuable as one taken in the cot.

Provided that he is able to fall asleep in his cot at the start of the night and for daytime naps reasonably often, allowing him to nap in his pram each day will not hamper his self-settling skills.

Most babies now sleep for between six and ten hours at night, with two to three daytime naps, totalling about 13–14 hours.

It is at this age that your baby will begin to respond to a bedtime routine. Look back to Chapter 2 for advice.

Four to six months: your baby's top sleep needs

- Plenty of stimulation during the day.
- Three to four daytime naps.
- The establishment of a consistent bedtime routine.
- Encouragement to fall asleep without feeding or being rocked in your arms.

The four-month sleep regression

Somewhere between about three and five months, babies have got their days and nights sorted out and will have settled into a mature pattern of sleep cycles, with light sleep, deep sleep and waking phases.

They will also now be producing their own supply of sleep hormones, (melatonin), and they may also have the body weight to enable them to sleep for stretches of five hours or more at night without getting hungry.

So, given that all this positive stuff is going on, it can be frustrating when babies start to go backwards with their sleeping. Why does this happen?

Between three and five months, babies become more conscious of what is going on and they start to make learning connections. These connections, especially if they are made at sleep onset, can develop into expectations and preferences around their night sleeping and napping. So as an example: if they are fed or cuddled to sleep at the start of the night, they may need those same 'sleep triggers' when they wake up naturally later.

Of course, it is fine to cuddle or feed your baby back to sleep if that's what feels right for you or if that's what they need, but bear in mind that if, at this age, your baby starts to wake for more feeds and cuddles than they used to, there is a good chance that they are doing so out of habit rather than need, and this can be really disruptive to their sleep and to yours, too.

When dealing with this problem, a good bedtime routine really comes into its own. You need a repeated series of steps leading up to bedtime that baby will recognize as sleep cues.

Then, unless you've chosen to co-sleep, it's good to help them fall asleep in the cot aware of where they are. A lovely way of doing this is to give the last feed with the light on and follow it with a little book. Then turn off the lights and put them down into the cot awake. Soothe them there if they don't like to be left, or leave them to self-settle if they're OK with that.

As sleep now happens in cycles, it is normal for babies to wake up a few times during sleep. When your baby wakes up, they will need to have everything around them, the same as it was when they fell asleep.

So, the more independently they fall asleep at the start of sleep, the more likely they are to be able to join their sleep cycles by themselves.

If your baby does wake up, try soothing him in the cot for a while rather than automatically picking him up or feeding him. Your baby might just resettle and drift back off, but of course, if he continues to cry, it is best to respond with whatever feeding or cuddling he needs.

Why do babies cry?

Before the development of speech, the primary way your baby has of communicating his needs to you is through crying. For lots of parents, hearing their baby cry can be stressful and worrying. Sometimes, it is possible to interpret the nature of your baby's cry and to be able to tell the difference between a hungry cry, a tired cry or a cry of discomfort, for example. This is not always the case, however, and it can be utterly demoralizing having a crying baby on your hands and not knowing how to comfort him. It is important to realize that, in these early weeks and months, picking your baby up, cuddling him and soothing him will not spoil him. He needs to know that if something is wrong, you are there to comfort and help him. By consistently responding to his needs when he is very little, you will build the foundations of trust and security that he needs in order to mature into independence.

It is completely normal for babies to cry *a lot* in the early weeks. Crying tends to start ramping up at about two weeks, peaks at about two months and then gradually gets less severe and tails off at around four months. This period of intense crying is sometimes called the 'crying curve'.

To establish why he is crying, use the checklist below.

My baby is crying. What might be wrong?

- Is he hungry? Try offering a feed. Even if he is not yet due for one, he may be having a growth spurt and need a little extra.
- Is he tired? Try putting him down to sleep.
- Does he have wind? Try holding him upright, supporting him firmly against your shoulder and applying firm circular strokes to his lower back until he manages to pass his wind.
- Is he too hot or too cold? Look for signs that he is sweating or cold. Feel his abdomen to get a rough idea of his body temperature. Check the room temperature – it should be around 18°C (64°F). Also, during the day, check that he and the pram or cot are not placed in direct sunlight.
- Does his nappy need changing?
- Is he being over-handled? Sometimes, if a baby is crying miserably, is restless and is difficult to comfort, it can be a sign that he is just tired and irritable. The best thing to do is put him in his cot or pram and allow him to settle by himself.
- Is he in pain? Check that his clothing is comfortable and not overtight, and then check him for wind and nappy rash. Look at his gums to see if he is cutting a tooth. If he is hot and/or crying inconsolably, if the nature of his cry is different compared to normal or if he is listless, you should seek immediate medical help.

Common medical reasons for excessive crying at this age include:

- colic or reflux
- teething
- nappy rash
- earache/infections.

These conditions, although challenging at the time, tend to be temporary and respond well to medicine prescribed by your GP. Of course, there are more serious illnesses that might account for your baby's excessive crying, and it needs to be stressed once more that, *if your baby is unsettled and seems in any way different from his normal self, you should always seek immediate medical help.*

Coping with a crying baby

It may be the case that your baby cries more than others do. You might have noticed that yours is the baby who cries the most during visits to the clinic, at baby groups and (especially stressful) as you try to do some shopping. On the other hand, it may be that your baby doesn't cry more than others but that you, as a parent, for whatever reason, find your baby's crying very stressful. If this describes you, you are by no means alone.

If you have gone through the above checklist and ruled out any physical cause for your baby's cries, try the following tips to learn how to deal with it.

Top tips: coping with crying

- Don't be afraid to hold and comfort your baby if that calms him.
- Try not to worry about getting behind with other jobs. Nothing is as important as your baby's needs. If ignoring other tasks makes you even more stressed, however, consider carrying your baby around with you in a very supportive sling, so that you can get on with what you need to do.

- Allow others to comfort him if they offer ... and try not to feel undermined if they succeed. Sometimes it is just the change of scene that helps.
- Try placing your baby in his cot, on his side with one of your hands in the small of his back and the other against his tummy. Gently rock him to and fro until he falls asleep and then reposition him on to his back.
- Remember: your baby is not crying on purpose. If you find yourself getting angry, put him in a safe place and leave him on his own for a few minutes while you walk away, have a little weep, take some deep breaths or telephone someone for moral support.
- Don't return to your baby if you feel angry; similarly, don't let your partner return to him if he or she is angry.
- Never shake your baby.
- Only return to your baby when you are calm.
- Make some time for yourself, even if it is just half an hour for a relaxing bath.
- Remember that this is a phase. It won't last for ever. It will soon get better.
- Talk to your family, partner, health visitor or GP if you feel that you are not coping.
- Ring the Cry-sis helpline (see 'Further help and resources' at the end of this book). Cry-sis is an organization that supports and advises the parents of crying babies.

How to settle a crying baby during the night

If your baby is under six months old and cries a lot at night, rather than going for one of the 'controlled crying' solutions (see Chapter 9) it is best to try some more gentle alternatives.

- The most important thing that you can do to prevent night-time waking and crying is always to place your baby in the cot after his bedtime feed while he is still awake and to settle him there rather than in your arms.

- If you are offering a 10–11 p.m. feed (also known as a 'dream feed'), it is important that your baby is awake when placed back in his cot after this feed, too, especially if he is over eight weeks old. The same goes for any later night or dawn feeds.

- If your baby's night-time cries are merely 'grumblings' and he is not yet due for a feed, you should briefly check that he is comfortable, warm enough but not too hot, and that his nappy is not sodden or soiled. If all these things are all right, you should encourage him to resettle in his cot after a reassuring cuddle.

If he continues to cry, try the tips below.

Top tips: what to do when your baby wakes in the night – settling tips for four- to six-month-olds

- Keep the lighting low and remain quiet as you resettle him. Do not attempt to entertain him or distract him with play. You need to offer a clear message that it is night-time.
- Pick him up and hold him closely and firmly against your shoulder in an upright position to help him bring up any trapped wind. Stroking the base of his back rather than patting his upper back is a more effective way of helping to bring relief.
- Place him on his side with one of your hands in the small of his back and the other against his tummy. Gently rock him to and fro until he resettles, then reposition him on to his back.
- Offer him a drink of water.
- Rock him in your arms, but as soon as he begins to calm down and become sleepy, place him back in his cot and comfort him there.
- Offer him a milk feed, but do not allow him to fall asleep while sucking. As soon as he has had enough or is starting to become sleepy, stop the feed, wind him well and then place him back in the cot. Comfort him there if you need to until he has gone to sleep.

I was 42 when I had Abigail, and she was so very precious to us. Even before I was pregnant, I used to visualize myself as a mother, holding my baby in my arms, playing games, feeding her, etc.

I had a difficult birth, but I loved Abigail on sight and bonded with her immediately. What I wasn't prepared for was the impact that her crying had on me. She was a colicky baby in those early weeks and sometimes I felt really helpless when I couldn't comfort her. In the evenings, she would cry and cry, but would refuse to be comforted by the breast. Sometimes she would become rigid in my arms, crying continuously. I felt like I was a hopeless mother and that I must be doing something wrong. I even began to suspect that Abigail didn't like me! Her constant crying made me feel tense and panicky. I began to be afraid of being with her, and the whole thing absolutely knocked my confidence.

She grew out of the colic when she was three months old, thank goodness, and I was able to feed her, hold her and comfort her as I had wanted to. She's a year old now and a delight to be with. I will never forget that difficult time, however, and I always feel sympathetic towards parents when I see them struggling to comfort a crying child.

Babies who will sleep only in your arms

Some babies are only happy and content when they are held in someone's arms and will cry whenever they are put down in the cot. We have already looked at how to cope with this during the daytime, but during the night it is both impractical and unsafe to have your baby strapped to you in a sling. It is exhausting having to spend the night pacing up and down the room, rocking him in your arms.

Babies need to feel both sleepy and safe in order to settle and sleep well at night. One way of achieving this, as we have already seen, is to follow a consistent bedtime routine.

Another way of helping your baby to feel safe and contained is to reproduce the feeling of your touch by artificial means.

One way of doing this is to use light swaddling. As discussed earlier, the gentle pressure of being wrapped mimics the feeling of being held. At this age, your baby might prefer to be swaddled just up to chest height, with his arms free. Alternatively, a light sheet tucked into either side of the cot can produce a light and reassuring pressure.

A baby's need to be held can prevent him from being able to settle and sleep for a sustained period. To maximize the sleep potential of a baby at this age who likes to be held close, use one of the above suggestions for reproducing your touch and then place him in the cot when you know he is tired. Stay beside him, with the additional soft pressure of your hand on his tummy until he ceases crying and goes to sleep. Over time, once he has got used to falling asleep in his cot, you can begin to withdraw your contact until he is able to go to sleep without help.

Top tips: settling four- to six-month-old babies who only like being held in your arms

- A bedtime massage can help to give her the sensory feedback as well as the lovely closeness that she needs.
- If you're using a sheet and blanket, stretching these firmly across her body at chest height and tucking them under the mattress will help her feel contained and secure.
- Using your arm, apply gentle pressure to her body as she lies in the cot.
- Play white noise continuously during the night.

Feeding at night – to feed or not to feed?

Your baby may still require a night feed up to age of a year, and it is fine to feed beyond that if you both enjoy it and it's not wrecking your sleep. However, if your baby is gaining weight correctly, is over about 13 lb (6 kg), is not unwell and decides to drop feeds by himself, it is absolutely fine to allow him to do so. It is also fine to nudge him in the direction of dropping the night feeds at this stage if you're struggling, if you feel that he is feeding only as a sleep trigger, or if he has started to take more frequent and shorter night feeds.

If you are still waking your baby for a 10–11 p.m. 'dream feed' at four months or more, you should think about stopping – especially if he is taking only a small amount or does not seem particularly interested. The reason for this is that, by establishing a milk/sleep connection, you may be unwittingly encouraging your baby to feed unnecessarily, not just at this time, but at other times during the night, when he stirs during the light phase of a sleep cycle.

Rather than wake him up, allow him to wake naturally for this feed and, when he does, offer an increasingly smaller feed, making sure that he doesn't fall fast asleep while taking it and before you place him back in his cot.

Insight

If your baby is waking for feeds more frequently than every three hours after the age of 12 weeks, he might be feeding more as a sleep trigger than out of hunger, and this could possibly lead to him developing a sleep problem.

As we will see in the coming chapters, sleep problems can sometimes be caused by nutritionally unneeded feeds and by feeding babies to make them sleep. Provided that you are able to put your baby back into his cot following his night feeds while he is *awake*, there is every chance that you will avoid later problems.

It is very important to hold your baby upright and wind him well after any night feeds, especially if he is formula-fed, is a 'windy' baby or has colic or reflux. This prevents him from being woken with a tummy ache later.

Top tips: night feeds

- After the age of eight weeks, discourage your baby from falling asleep over a night feed.
- Make sure that, when the feed is finished, your baby is aware that he has been put back in his cot.
- Do not try to drop night breast feeds in the early weeks. Night feeds ensure that you establish a good supply of milk.
- Always wind your baby well after a feed.
- Feed him in a comfortable chair next to his cot rather than in your bed.
- Stop the 'dream feed' after four months if your baby is gaining weight nicely.

Case study

Ten-week-old baby girl: unsettled during the day and sleeping badly at night

Carla was a formula-fed baby, was feeding well and gaining weight nicely. At times, she was a happy, smiling baby... but not always.

The problem

Carla was restless and irritable at times during the day. She took frequent short naps and often woke up crying, appearing still to be tired. During the night she was feeding very small amounts every two hours or more. She would only ever go to sleep if she was held and rocked in one of her parents' arms.

The solution

1. Carla needed to regulate her daytime sleep routine and learn to settle more independently.
2. She also needed to drop any unnecessary night feeds.

The sleep plan

Daytime

- Aim for three to four daytime naps, with awake windows of around two hours.
- When at home, settle her in her cot, but, if it suits, once a day allow her to sleep while out in her pram.
- Schedule naps approximately two hours after each feed but use this schedule as a rough guide only. It is better to work with Carla's

natural tendency for sleep rather than impose a schedule that doesn't suit her needs.

- Having given her her first feed at 7 a.m., at around 9 a.m. observe Carla for signs of tiredness – that is, yawning, rubbing eyes, becoming grumpy. Before she becomes overtired, take her to her cot, draw the bedroom curtains and, instead of rocking her to sleep, put her down while she is awake.
- Once she is in her cot, stay beside her, patting her if necessary until she settles to sleep.
- If she wakes up after less than an hour, go back to her and pat her again for up to 20 minutes. If she goes back to sleep, leave her until she wakes up naturally. If she is unable to go back to sleep, abandon resettling her, get her up, give her her next bottle a little early but do not allow her to fall asleep during it. Then settle her for her next nap up to an hour earlier than its due time.
- Give her her second feed of the day sometime between 10.30 and 11 a.m. The fact that she has napped prior to this feed will enable her to have the energy to feed well and enjoy her milk.
- Around two hours later, take her out in the pram for her lunchtime nap. (Babies tend to enjoy napping on the move, and it gives you some space, a little exercise and even the chance for a peaceful cup of coffee.)
- If necessary, give Carla her 3 p.m. bottle while out and about.
- Offer a final, shorter nap at home in her cot at around 5 p.m. Settle her in the same way as for the morning nap.

Bedtime

- On waking at around 5.30 p.m., Carla should have a little play time. By 6 p.m., give her half of her bedtime bottle while still downstairs. (The reason for this is that by bedtime she was often so tired that she fell asleep over her bottle and couldn't manage a full feed.)
- Begin her bedtime routine around one and a half to two hours after she has woken from her final daytime nap.
- Bath her every night and, while doing this, sing the same song.
- Use familiar phrases at key stages during the routine, such as when she enters the bedroom. These phrases will in time become a series of little sleep triggers.
- After the bath, go directly to the bedroom to put her night clothes on. Once ready, offer her the second half of her bottle, sitting close by the cot.

- Keep a soft light on in the room and do not allow her to fall asleep while taking this feed.
- After the feed, wind her well; during this process, hold her upright and sing a little bedtime song. It needs to be the same song each night to give Carla a feeling of safety and familiarity.
- Then turn the lights down or off and place her in her cot while awake. If necessary, comfort her there until she falls asleep. As she becomes accustomed to falling asleep in her cot, gradually withdraw the amount of patting until you are just sitting quietly beside her as she falls asleep.
- When Carla is able to go to sleep without being patted, you need to move gradually out of the room until she is able to settle to sleep without you.

During the night

- Go to bed as early as you can and divide the night into shifts, so that each of you can be sure of getting some rest.
- Do not wake Carla for her 11 p.m. bottle, as you have been doing, but wait for her to wake of her own accord and feed her then.
- This feed should be given sitting beside the cot rather than in your bed. After it, Carla should be winded, put back into her cot while still awake and then settled there as she had been at the start of the night.
- If she wakes up again before 5 a.m., she should be offered a drink of water only and settled in her cot as before.
- At any waking between 5 and 6 a.m. she can be offered a 3-oz (90-ml) bottle of milk, provided that she doesn't fall asleep and is put into her cot afterwards. This is to encourage her to sleep on until 7 a.m.
- If she has taken this small dawn feed, expect her to take less milk than normal at her first daytime feed.

The outcome

Carla's parents were able to help her sleep through the night in less than ten days and with minimal crying. For the first two nights that they dropped her 'dream feed', she did not wake up until 2 a.m. She fed well and then resettled from awake with minimal help. She stirred briefly both mornings at 5.30 a.m. and was settled by patting only and then woke for the day at 6.45 a.m. On the third night, she did not wake for her bottle until 5.00 a.m., and they just gave her 3 oz (90 ml) of milk. She settled very easily and woke for the day at 7.15 a.m. This became a pattern for the next few nights until they decided to try just patting her at 5.30 a.m.

It took two mornings of patting her for half an hour for her to resettle, but soon after that she was back to waking up at around 7 a.m.

Her daytime sleep improved enormously, too, due to her improved self-settling skills. She soon settled into a pattern of a one-and-a-half-hour nap in the morning, followed by a two-hour nap in the early afternoon and then a half-hour nap at teatime. Because she was well rested during the day, she was happier and she fed better, too. This meant that she was able to enjoy her bedtime routine and her night-time bottle.

Conclusion

By removing the link between feeding and sleeping and by teaching Carla to go to sleep alone, her parents were able to dramatically improve her sleep skills. They were delighted that they had not had to leave her to cry alone to achieve this. *By addressing the cause of a baby's sleep difficulties, it is rarely necessary to use harsh sleep training methods.*

Ten things to remember

1. Breastfed babies may require night feeds for a little longer than formula-fed babies.
2. Breast milk is digested more quickly and easily than formula so babies might not go so long between feeds.
3. It is very important for good sleeping that babies are winded well after feeding and before being put to bed at night.
4. When your baby is a few weeks old and becoming more alert, you should discourage him from falling asleep on the breast or bottle.
5. If you are giving a 'dream feed', you should consider dropping it by four months.
6. The composition of breast milk changes towards the end of the day to contain higher levels of a natural sleep aid, tryptophan.
7. Swaddling and sensitive positioning can help your baby feel safe and secure when you are not there.
8. Giving a night breast feed helps to ensure that you have a plentiful milk supply for the following day.
9. Introduce a night-time or spoken ritual before settling your baby to sleep. It will become a portable sleep trigger.
10. By the age of six months, your baby should always be placed in his cot awake at the start of the night.

4

Sleep advice for six- to 12-month-old babies

Your baby may still seem very little to you, but by six months old, provided that she is gaining weight and is healthy, she almost certainly has the ability to sleep through the night. So what is stopping her?

We have seen already that, by six months old, babies are likely to have settled into a mature pattern of 90-minute sleep cycles. While, for many of them, this heralds a time of more peaceful nights, for others, it can mean that there are more definite wake-up periods during the night. For those babies who have learned good settling skills early on, this rarely presents a problem. However, for those whose sleep skills may still be a little fragile, hitting six months can signal a real deterioration in sleep.

In addition to the natural change in sleep structure, six months is the age at which certain physical and developmental changes can have an adverse effect on a baby's sleep. These factors include:

- teething
- becoming more mobile
- separation anxiety
- introduction of solid food.

Insight
Most babies of six months upwards no longer require a night feed and can be helped to sleep through the night.

Teething

The average age for a baby to cut her first tooth is around six months. For some babies, this occurs earlier, while others will have to wait for a year or more before teeth appear. Lots of babies have only very minor discomfort during teething (if any at all), but just as many really suffer during this time. One thing is for sure, however: most babies become grumpy and unsettled during this time and most will need some form of painkilling medicine at some point. For advice on managing your baby's teething problems, see Chapter 7.

Becoming more mobile

By the age of six months, many babies are able to roll over. Unfortunately, there is often a period of a couple of weeks or more before they learn how to roll back again. Many parents experience a worrying and tiring time at this stage, when they have to get up several times in the night, repositioning their baby who has got stuck in an awkward position. The good news is that, although it might feel never-ending, this developmental phase rarely lasts for more than a week or two. Once your baby can confidently roll on to her front and back again, you will not need to be up in the night constantly checking her position.

> Rosalind had slept well from about the age of three months. However, just after she was six months old, she began to cry out in the night, almost in panic. When we went to check on her, she was invariably stuck face down, in an awkward position and couldn't get herself right again. We were absolutely terrified, as we knew that it was safest for her to sleep on her back. We even thought she might suffocate.
>
> At first, one of us would pick her up and comfort her in our arms until she fell asleep and then we would put her down on her back again. This worked for a while, but we were often woken later to find Ros in the same awkward position. We

spoke to our health visitor, who reassured us that this was a phase that would soon pass. She advised us to go to Ros as soon as we heard her cry out and to reposition her in her cot rather than getting her out and rocking her back to sleep.

This worked very well for us. We decided to divide the night into two parts. One of us was to be on 'Ros duty' between 7 p.m. and 2 a.m. and the other one would take over until 7 a.m. This meant that, even though the sleep of both of us might be disturbed, each of us would get some uninterrupted rest in bed.

Thankfully, this phase did not last for very long, as Rosalind soon got the hang of settling herself into a comfortable position and sleeping through the night again. The advice from The Lullaby Trust is that once a baby can roll both ways, if they choose to sleep on their front, it is OK to let them.

The next stage in your baby's mobility comes when she is able to either sit up or climb on to all fours. Suddenly, it becomes more difficult to keep her in the lying-down position if she wakes during the night. What begins as a cuddle and an attempt to lay her back down can turn into a rugby tackle and pin-down. Her ability to move around and especially to get up when she rouses in her sleep will wake her further. When you go in to attend to her and find her sitting or kneeling in her cot rather than lying down, you can be sure that it is going to take some time before she resettles. Once again, provided that you do not get into the habit of rocking or feeding her back to sleep, it will very quickly pass.

Then, as your baby approaches her first birthday, she will learn how to stand up in her cot. Suddenly, you may be aware of her not just crying, but often calling and rattling the cot bars, too!

What do I do if my baby won't lie down?

It is important, when your child sits, kneels or stands up in the cot, that you show her how to lie down, get comfortable and go to sleep. First, you should physically place her into a good sleeping position again. If she immediately springs back up, you need to choose your approach.

Option 1

Rather than keep tackling her back down, just place your hands reassuringly on her (or around her if she is standing up) and hold her as she is standing. Lay her down every two to five minutes and expect her to get back up again at first. She will eventually run out of steam and remain laying down.

As soon as she does lie down, you should reward her by praising her warmly. Stay beside her until she has gone to sleep. By using this gentle approach, she will learn how to resettle and reposition herself with your support rather than your direct intervention.

Option 2

Reposition her and reassure her briefly before leaving the room. Still leave the room even if she is standing up or kneeling before you get to the door. Return to her every two to five minutes for the briefest period, just to lay her back down. Reinforce your actions by saying, 'Lie down now' in a calm, non-aggressive voice. Each time you reposition her, try not to get into a physical tussle with her and do not hold her down. It is more important that she lies down than that she stays down. Staying down will come later, when she gets tired – and gets the message. By using this firmer approach, your baby will learn to settle back to sleep by receiving a very clear message that you expect her to lie down in the cot.

As soon as your baby is able to sit, stand or kneel in the cot, you need to lower its base to the bottom setting and get rid of any bumper. These measures are to prevent her from toppling out of the cot. The bumper, if firmly fitted, can potentially provide her with a step-up to climb over the cot side.

Tiffany had never been a great sleeper, but my mum had told me that, when she became more active, she would wear herself out and start to sleep better. I had really looked forward to the time when she started crawling, but unfortunately this was when things started to go from bad to worse.

Being more active certainly tired her out – so much so that she rarely managed to finish her night-time bottle before she crashed out in my arms. She would sleep deeply until about 2 a.m. when she would wake up, pull herself up and stand holding the top of the cot side. She cried as if her heart would break. The first few times this happened, I would lift her out of the cot and hold her in my arms until she calmed down and went back to sleep. Then I could put her back into her cot. More often than not, she would wake again and I would have to go through the same process to get her to go back to sleep. After a time, she began to really struggle to go back to sleep, and at that point I started to bring her into bed with us.

Finally, we all managed to get some sleep! Before long, though, she began refusing to go into her cot at the beginning of the night, and during the night she was very fidgety. It got to the point where we were all exhausted, and I knew that I had to do something about it.

We were advised to make sure that Tiffany was awake when we put her in her cot at night. If she stood up, we were to leave her standing, cheerfully say goodnight, exit the room but come back into it every five minutes. Each time we went back to her, we were to lay her down gently and praise her when she was in the lying-down position before leaving her again. Because she was so active, she was exhausted at bedtime and we actually only needed to go back in to her three times before she went off to sleep.

On the first night, she woke just after 2 a.m., standing up as usual. We responded by laying her down again, as we did at the beginning of the night. She must have known what to do, because she went straight back to sleep. I couldn't believe how easy it was, and I'm kicking myself that we waited so long before tackling her sleep issue.

Sometimes, it is not possible to leave your child to cry alone. It may be that you feel instinctively it is wrong or just that you are afraid of disturbing others in the family or even neighbours. The good news is that gradual withdrawal techniques work just as well, provided that you have a clear plan and follow it to its conclusion.

Our problems with Joshua's sleep began after a bout of teething, when he had got used to having medicine and cuddles in the night.

Even when he was no longer teething or poorly, he would wake in the early hours, almost as if it was a habit. He didn't just cry when he woke up; he screamed! The moment I picked him up, he would stop crying and settle to sleep in my arms. I knew that I had to get him used to staying in his cot again, but it was so difficult as, when he woke up, he was invariably sitting or kneeling, crying and bashing the cot. I didn't want to leave him alone to cry, as it seemed too harsh. Just a few nights before, I had spent so much time soothing him in my arms and I thought he might feel hurt and confused by the change in my attitude towards him.

I decided to try the gentle approach, where my task was to keep him in his cot, help him to get comfortable, but not force him to lie down if he didn't want to, and to stay beside him, giving whatever comfort I felt was necessary. Over the coming nights, as Joshua became accustomed to staying in his cot, I was to gradually withdraw from him until he was sleeping independently again. He protested so much on that first night that I thought he might be sick. It was horrible, but I knew that he was feeling frustrated rather than abandoned. I did not force him to lie down if he didn't want to, but stayed beside him, holding his hand. Each time he made a move to lie down, I praised him warmly.

On the third night, he lay immediately back down the moment I walked into his room and I knew that I was getting somewhere. Soon after that, I cut the amount of time that I stayed beside him and also stopped holding his hand. By the fifth night, I knew that he no longer expected me to get him out of his cot and cuddle him back to sleep, so after checking him briefly when he woke up, I left him to settle alone. He cried for about half an hour, but his cry was more of a 'grumble'. It was completely different from the intense screaming he was doing at the start of the week. I felt OK about leaving him to cry at this point and, in fact, he has not woken in the night since.

I have always felt uneasy about sleep training, and I know I'm a bit of a softy, but I believe the whole process has not harmed Josh in the slightest. He is still his normal sunny self during the day, and he sleeps like a dream at night.

Separation anxiety

Insight

Newborn babies think that they and their mother are one and the same person.

When she is around seven to eight months old, you may notice that your baby becomes upset when you leave the room. Prior to this, she may have been happy for you to be around but not over-stressed when she couldn't see you.

Similarly, when she was very little, she will have found that being passed to another adult, even if that person was a stranger, was no problem to her. Suddenly, at this age, she will cry when she is held by another person whom she doesn't know very well, even if you are close by.

This is an absolutely normal stage in her development and not at all a sign that she is emotionally fragile in any way. It is a fact that a new baby thinks that she is part of her mother. At first, she has no sense that she is an individual. It takes time for her to realize that she is a separate person and not one and the same as her mummy.

This realization tends to occur at around eight months old, and it usually brings with it a real sense of anxiety. Your baby will demonstrate this by becoming clingy and upset when you leave her. By now, she understands the concept of 'object permanence' (that is, when she throws a toy from her cot, she knows that it continues to exist even though she can't see it), so she knows that you will come back to her. What makes her anxious is that she has no real sense of time yet. If you leave the room even for a moment, she has no idea when you are coming back.

Clearly, this has huge implications for sleep training your baby. No parent wants their child to feel fearful and anxious, especially at night. Unfortunately, there are no magical solutions to dealing with this difficult time, but there are some measures that you can take in order to help your baby feel more secure about being apart from you.

Top tips: helping your anxious baby

- Play 'peek-a-boo' games with her, where you hide first of all behind a newspaper, then behind a piece of furniture and finally behind a door. Keep your disappearances brief and your reappearances loving, with lots of cuddling.
- Before leaving her with another caregiver, make time for a relaxed and lengthy settling-in period. You should be present for as much of this time as you can.
- If you intend to leave your child with a nursery or childminder, try to schedule this before the separation anxiety starts or once it has finished.
- When you are in another room, chat to yourself or sing, so that, even though she can't see you, she can hear you.
- Conscientiously follow familiar daytime and evening rituals, so that she feels safe and secure.
- Never leave her in the care of others without saying goodbye to her. Sneaking away will only increase her anxiety in future.
- If you are back at work, make the most of your time with her before you leave in the morning and especially when you return at night.

Separation anxiety can last anything between a few weeks and several months and may have an impact on your baby's sleep. Even if you have managed to avoid problems at six months when her sleep developed into the mature sleep-cycle pattern, there is still a chance that you may encounter problems at the seven-months-plus point.

No form of sleep training should be traumatic for a baby, no matter how tempting the benefits of unbroken nights are. Psychologically, it is better for your baby either to remain close to you during this period of separation anxiety or to experience only very sensitive, gentle and gradual training.

Top tips: sensitive sleep training

- Follow a highly consistent bedtime routine, to help her feel safe.
- Be especially close, loving and physically warm with your baby when preparing her for bed.
- At bedtime, make sure that she is in a safe place, then pop in and out of the bedroom briefly – to bring her nightclothes, for instance. Be cheerful and calm each time you return.
- After a familiar story and goodnight ritual, place her into her cot while she is still awake, then stay beside her until she goes to sleep. Gradually move yourself away from the cot over a period of a week or two until she feels secure being in her room alone.
- If you decide to leave her to settle alone from the start, return to her briefly and frequently to reassure her. Act like your normal self when you go in to her. It will unsettle her if you avoid eye contact and voice contact with her and will only make her feel more anxious.
- After a night of sleep training, be especially responsive to her on the following day.

When Aiden was six months old, I returned to work. I found it very hard to leave him as I had enjoyed every moment of his life and was anxious about how his childminder would fill my shoes. At first, he was fine and I really felt that I had got the 'work–life balance' sorted. After a few weeks, however, he became very clingy towards me and cried whenever I moved more than a few feet away from him. He was OK with his childminder but would avoid other new adults. Previously, he had been happy to go to sleep in his cot alone at the beginning of the night, but all of that suddenly changed. I found that I had to hold him close to me to get him off to sleep and then he would wake up with real tears looking for me during the night. I was absolutely sure that I had caused this anxiety by returning to work, and if we hadn't needed the money, I would have handed in my notice immediately.

On talking to other mothers in my post-natal group, I found that most of them were experiencing similar issues with their babies. Some of us were back at work and some were staying at home, but whatever the circumstances, all the babies were becoming clingy. I know it's awful, but I felt so much better! I did some reading and found that Aiden's behaviour was typical of a baby with normal separation anxiety and that I was not to blame. This made me feel much more confident, and I knew that, in time, he would be all right. His behaviour lasted for maybe three months, and I'm glad to say that he is fine now, back to his easy-going self.

Top tip

Don't automatically blame your baby's increased anxiety on the fact that you've returned to work. At seven months plus, this was likely to have happened anyway.

Why won't my baby sleep in her cot?

It is usually between six and 12 months that your baby makes her needs and wants very clear to you. For many families, this is the time when a baby firmly entrenches herself into the parental bed. A combination of your baby teething, standing up and crying in the cot and of your own worry or guilt over your baby's separation anxiety and, to be honest, your own tiredness and exasperation can make you take the line of least resistance and bring her into bed with you. While there is no doubt that this might bring some initial relief in that you all get some sleep at least, the quality of that sleep is often poor and, over time, everyone can end up exhausted.

It is a fact that babies fidget and wriggle during the night. They also sleep horizontally across the pillows and have absolutely no regard for the well-being of their parents, who invariably end up sleeping so close to the edge that they are hanging half in and half out of the bed by morning. Parents who share their bed with their baby often suffer from stiff necks, bad backs and bad moods.

On a more serious note, sleeping in your bed is not recommended for safety reasons. Not only this, but over time the initial benefits of having your baby sleep with you can end up working against you. Often, babies who get into this habit will struggle to settle in their own cots at the start of the night, too.

Top tips: how to help your baby sleep all night in her cot

- Help her to settle in her cot at the start of the night.
- Help her to overcome the expectation that she will transfer to your bed during the night.
- Teach her that her cot is a safe and permanent sleeping place.

Case study
Seven-month-old baby boy: feeding to sleep and sleeping in his parents' bed

The problem
Leo was a well-grown baby who was enjoying solids and developing well. At bedtime, he was settled to sleep with a breast feed and was then transferred to his cot. He would wake up any time from half an hour to two hours later in a very upset state. The only way that he could be comforted was by being breastfed back to sleep. At each waking, he would become increasingly difficult to settle, until his

parents moved him into their bed in the early hours of the morning. Here he would settle but continue to breastfeed frequently during the night.

The reason

It is perfectly normal for babies to wake at night. Leo's difficulties were down to the fact that he was unable to resettle without help. His parents thought that the reason for his frequent feeding was because he was a hungry baby. A vicious cycle had been established whereby Leo fed little during the day because he was so used to feeding during the night. His parents needed to be reassured that he would be able to establish a better feeding pattern and that his night feeds were being used mainly as sleep prompts.

They also learned that Leo was not yet able to accept his cot as a safe and permanent sleeping place. This was because he only ever went into it when he was asleep. Each time he woke, he felt alarmed to find himself in a strange place and he cried. The natural response of his parents was to remove him from his cot and bring him to their bed, where he was comforted and fed back to sleep. He had learned that the right and proper place for his sleep was in bed with his mum and dad!

The solution

To help Leo sleep through the night, the family needed him to:
- fall asleep in his cot at the beginning of the night, aware of where he was
- drop his night breast feeds and lose his suck/sleep dependence
- overcome the expectation of transferring to his mum and dad's bed and to learn that his cot was his safe and permanent sleeping place.

The plan

- Establish a lovely consistent bedtime routine. This will provide Leo with a clear series of steps leading up to bedtime. In a very short time, each of these steps will become sleep cues.
- Incorporate familiar phrases and songs into the routine, as these are very effective as well as highly portable cues. A good routine will not only help Leo to feel sleepy but also to feel safe.
- The ideal time to begin the routine is around two to three hours after he has woken from his last daytime nap.
- After his nightly bath, take him directly to his room for his final feed. The room should be softly but well lit.

- You need to limit the duration of the feed to prevent him dozing, as it is very important that he is awake when he has finished.
- After the feed, while Leo is still awake, one of you should hold him in your arms and then together look at a simple picture book for a few moments. If you keep to the same one each night, it will become a sleep prompt for him.
- After the story, turn down the light and say goodnight to him. Regardless of whether or not he is still wide awake, you should place him in his cot.

Nights 1 and 2

- One of you should kneel or sit next to the cot and stroke his chest (or his back if he is kneeling up). As he eventually gives in to sleep, you should just have a hand resting on him.
- You should stay beside him, patting and stroking him if he needs you to until he eventually gives in to sleep. It is OK to speak softly, using repetitive phrases, or to hum to him.
- Demonstrating a confident and calm demeanour will really help Leo to feel safe. It is best not to lift him out of his cot, but, if you have to, place him back down once he is calm but still awake. There is no need to leave him alone, at this stage. Your first aim is to allow him to go to sleep in his cot, without the breast in his mouth. It is important not to be alarmed when he cries, as he is merely protesting at the change. He is also expressing his frustration at wanting to go to sleep, but not being able to yet. This is what you are teaching him now.
- Eventually, he will give in to sleep but this may take an hour or more. As he goes to sleep, you should try not to be touching him, although it is OK for one of you to be beside him. In time, when he has learned how to sleep without sucking, you should withdraw your presence so that he learns to sleep independently.
- When Leo wakes before 10 p.m., it should be relatively easy to resettle him in his cot without feeding him or getting him out for a cuddle. You should offer him the same patting or stroking as you did at the beginning of the night.
- Each time he wakes up after 10 p.m., you can feed him in order to calm him and to address any possible learned hunger. You must, however, cut the duration of the night feeds to five minutes maximum. This is to prevent him from going to sleep on the breast and to wean him off having significant amounts of milk in his tummy during the night.

- After each night feed, place him back into his cot while he is still awake. You should expect some more crying, and it is fine to stay beside him if he needs you to. Even though it is stressful, you should keep calm and resolute – he is learning all the time.
- Following this approach, most babies spontaneously stop waking up for night feeds and will sleep through the night.

Nights 3 and 4

It is likely that, by now, Leo will settle down willingly when placed into his cot. If he wants you to stroke him, you can do so, but cut down on the duration. You should also try to reduce eye contact with him as he enters sleep, and should not be touching him at all.

During the night, you should continue to withhold feeds before 10 p.m. but now restrict any later feeds to three minutes maximum.

Night 5 onwards

- After placing Leo in his cot at the beginning of the night, and sitting next to him for a moment or two, you should begin to gently potter around the room. After a short time, you need to leave the room. If he calls out or cries, you should go back to him briefly to reassure and reposition him. You should not lift him out of the cot. After this, you need to leave him again, regardless of whether he is calm and then return to him every five minutes. It is not necessary to go back to him if he merely 'grumbles' or cries in a rhythmic or 'fussing' way. By now, as he is used to his cot and to going to sleep without the breast, this kind of cry is not a sign of any real distress. In time, the crying will become almost tuneful and is a natural prelude to sleep in many babies.
- During the night, Leo should not be fed at all when he wakes up. You can offer a little water but, provided he has had enough to drink during the day, it is unlikely that he will be thirsty.
- You should treat any night waking with the same consistent response that you have used at the start of the night – that is, returning briefly to reassure but not feed or pick up.
- Very soon he will take more food during the day to compensate for the lost night feeds, and the balance will be redressed.
- Throughout the plan, demonstrate a calm, loving and resolute manner.

The outcome

Once Leo's parents understood the reason for his frequent waking and feeding, they felt confident about tackling his sleep problem. They were relieved that they did not have to leave him alone to cry.

At the beginning of the very first night of sleep training, Leo cried for half an hour. After this, however, he slept in his cot for a four-and-a-half-hour stretch, which was far longer than he had ever done. He still, however, woke another two times in the night and was resettled back in his cot after the recommended short feeds. There was little or no crying when he went in his cot. Although the two short feeds were hard going, Leo's mum was used to having very little sleep and now realized that she was using her time with him during the night in a much more positive way. On the fourth night of the plan, Leo's mother stopped feeding him altogether. Instead, she went to him, repositioned and reassured him and then left him to resettle without her. Given that he now had the skills to sleep without the breast in his mouth and was no longer expecting to go into their bed, Leo settled very quickly.

On the fifth night, his parents were delighted that Leo slept through the night from 7 p.m. until 7.30 a.m. He has managed to maintain his good sleep habits, and the family now enjoy peaceful nights.

Conclusion

By understanding the reasons for Leo's sleep difficulties and breaking the solution down into manageable tasks, his parents were able to solve the problems effectively and with minimal trauma.

Introducing solids

For the first six months of your baby's life, all of her nutritional needs can be met with either breast milk or formula. She even has her own in-built stock of iron which will last her until she begins on solids. In the past, the weaning of babies happened much earlier, but in recent years we have learned that early weaning is not only unnecessary, but can sometimes also be unsafe, as your baby's body may not be mature enough to cope with foods other than milk.

If your baby has had digestive difficulties such as colic, allergies, food intolerances or reflux, you need to give careful consideration to the timing and method of weaning. Always follow the advice of your doctor, health visitor or dietician. Sometimes, introducing solid food to vulnerable babies can actually worsen, rather than alleviate, a sleep problem. This is due to tummy ache, diarrhoea or a worsening of allergic skin conditions such as eczema.

However, if your baby has already learned good self-settling skills and is taking just one small feed during the night before resettling and sleeping until the morning, the chances are that introducing solids might help her to sleep through the night.

Insight

You may think that introducing solids early will improve your baby's sleep, but this is not usually true. Babies who are exclusively milk fed will sleep through the night by six months when they are big enough and have learned independent settling skills.

Bethany had never been a brilliant sleeper, but I thought that when she began taking solid food her sleep would improve.

I introduced baby rice early, at four and a half months, and she loved it. She seemed to want to take more than the two teaspoons which was recommended for her. This confirmed to me that she was hungry, and that this was the reason for her needing to feed during the night. I gave the rice during the afternoon, so that her tummy was nice and full for bedtime.

When I came to give her her 7 p.m. bottle she was not so interested, and instead of her usual 8 oz (235 ml), she only took 5 oz (145 ml). This concerned me a bit, but I realized that she might not be so hungry because of the baby rice she had taken earlier. That night, I won't say that she slept any worse than normal, but she certainly didn't sleep any better.

It was only after I saw a sleep specialist that I realized that the reason for Bethany's sleep problem was not that she was hungry.

She was very well fed really, but her problem was that I used to feed her to sleep at the start of the night. When she woke in the night, the only way that she would settle was by taking another bottle. I'd always presumed that this was because she was hungry, but I came to realize that she fed not out of hunger but as a means of getting off to sleep. Once I taught her how to go to sleep without the bottle at the beginning of the night, she no longer needed it when she woke up during the night. I carried on giving the solids once I had started, but I can see in retrospect that I needn't have started her so early.

For advice on early weaning foods, consult your health visitor or look at some of the many excellent books available on the subject. From a sleep point of view, it is better to introduce solid food initially during the mid-morning period. This way, if there is any danger of the food causing an adverse reaction, there is time for it to get out of your baby's system before bedtime. There is nothing to be gained by filling your baby up with solid food just before bed. She will still benefit from the increased calorie and nutritional input, even if the food was given early in the day.

When do I know that my baby is ready for solid food?

- If she has been previously sleeping through the night, but is suddenly more wakeful and difficult to settle
- If she begins to show an interest in the food that you are eating
- If she drains her bottles and is unable to make it to the next feed without getting hungry
- If she can hold her head up and sit up straight with minimal support
- If you notice that her weight gain has dipped below her normal percentile line

From the time that Michael was very small, we had established a very consistent bedtime routine. By three months old, he was able to settle to sleep by himself, and he would always sleep well until we woke him for a feed at 10 p.m. He would take his milk very well and then generally sleep through until 4 a.m. We then gave another feed, and he would sleep until 7 a.m. At about four months old, he stopped waking for his 4 a.m. feed. Instead, he would wake at 6 and have a little water, which helped him go through until morning. At four and a half months, we stopped offering the 10 p.m. feed, as he really didn't seem to be interested in it anymore. From then on, he would sleep from 7 p.m. to 7 a.m. each night and we were the envy of all our friends.

Just before he was six months old, however, he began to wake at about 3 a.m. and was impossible to resettle. In desperation, we offered him a bottle of milk, which he demolished. We had read enough about sleep issues to know that he did not need the feed out of sheer habit; we knew that it was real hunger. If we needed a sign that it was time to introduce solid food, this was it. The following day, we gave him some baby rice and he really loved it. We carried on with our good sleep-settling practices and continued giving Michael baby rice during the day. Within a week he was sleeping through the night again.

We have always felt that, by being sensitive to the signals Michael gives us, we haven't gone far wrong, and following his lead on when to start solids has confirmed to us that this is the best way.

Daytime naps between six and 12 months

During this time of rapid growth and development, napping is very important for your baby. The average for daytime sleep at this age is two naps a day totalling two to three and a half hours. However, some babies may take three naps and others just one. Difficulties arise when your baby takes very frequent, short and reluctant naps. Often, babies who do this will sleep for hours if they are in the pram or in your arms. Clearly, this is not always practical or even desirable. At times, even the most selfless of parents needs a little space during the day.

From your baby's point of view, you need to remember that, at this age, she is constantly being bombarded with new sights and experiences, not to mention discovering her own new skills and abilities. The world is a fascinating place, full of wonder and challenges, and she is using up masses of energy in discovering it. If she is to appreciate and enjoy all this newness, she needs at regular intervals to step back, have a rest and then start again afresh. If she doesn't do this, she will end up overtired and overstimulated. This will lead to tears and irritability, which can even affect the way that she sleeps at night.

For many babies, being well rested during the day means that they will sleep better at night.

> Simone had never been easy to settle for her daytime naps, but we thought that, when she became mobile, she would be so exhausted that she would be easier to settle. In fact, she got even worse! We could see that she was tired, as she was so cranky and kept crying and rubbing her eyes, but as soon as we put her in her cot she would be hysterical. The only way that we could get her to sleep was by putting her in the car and driving around with her. I couldn't always do this, as there were times that my husband needed the car for work.

> When she was about eight or nine months old, her night-time sleep got worse, too. Soon we found that she hardly slept (if at all) during the day and then was up in the night several times, only to start the day at 5 a.m. We worked out that she was getting a total of only about ten hours' sleep every 24 hours.

> The funny thing was that she didn't seem to be tired, actually. She was very active and into everything. Looking back, though, I realize that at this time she was very irritable indeed. I think that she was overtired and struggling – just as I was!

Does this sound familiar? It is all too easy for babies to get into a vicious circle, where lack of sleep during the day leads to unsettled nights. Given that we know that babies who do not get enough sleep become *extra active* rather than lethargic and sleepy, this wound-up tiredness leads to an inability to relax and nap during the following day and so the pattern is repeated.

The best way to break this pattern is to begin by optimizing your baby's sleep skills at *night*. This might seem the wrong way around, but, in fact, at night your baby is biologically 'programmed' to sleep – she is surrounded by other sleep prompts, there has been a build-up of sleep hormones and sleep pressure, and there has more chance of a 'wind-down' time. It may help if you give her an earlier bedtime, so that she is not totally exhausted and her cortisol levels are not so high. In this way, with all the balls in her court, you can then help her to fall asleep alone, knowing that you are close by.

It is absolutely tempting after an exhausting day with an active baby to allow her to fall asleep over her milk feed or be rocked in your arms until she is at the point of sleep. If you do this, however, it will soon begin to work against you, and she will wake up later looking for you. Not only this, but if she crashes to sleep in your arms at bedtime due to sheer exhaustion, she has no opportunity to develop the settling skills that she needs for her daytime naps.

You might think that your baby goes into her cot while awake, but ask yourself if she *really knows* that you are no longer beside her.

Working with her to encourage self-settling needs to be done at the beginning of the night, rather than if she wakes up during the night. This is because, at this time, she is more likely to succeed. Once she has gone to sleep by herself, she is more likely to sleep for a longer period. You need her to have had a good night's sleep and be well rested and not overtired if you are to help her nap well during the day. Don't be discouraged, however, if when you begin to teach her how to fall asleep alone she still wakes in the night. This will soon stop, but in the meantime, consider these wakings as an opportunity to reinforce the good settling skills that you are teaching her. Look at Chapter 9 for practical help on teaching your baby to sleep alone.

Once you have helped your baby to fall asleep at bedtime, she will then, provided that she has not become overtired, have the skills and ability to fall asleep for her naps.

Case study

Nine-month-old baby boy: refusing daytime naps and needing to be rocked or fed to sleep at night

Morton had a five-year-old sister, Iris. He was a healthy baby, who was feeding well on formula and solids and was growing well. He was happy and responsive and had recently started to crawl.

The problem

Morton had recently begun to refuse to go into his cot for daytime sleeps. This meant that he was often irritable, crying and needing to be carried around in his mother's arms when awake. He would only ever go to sleep when he was being pushed in his pram or when in the car, and even then he would try to resist sleep. When he did manage to go to sleep, he woke after just half an hour, crying and rubbing his eyes. Despite appearing to be tired, it was impossible to get him to go back to sleep.

In addition to this, Morton was becoming very difficult to settle at bedtime. He was clearly overtired, but unable to relax and let go into sleep. This meant that his mother had begun to feed him to sleep in the dark in his room, and if he didn't fall asleep on his bottle, she would rock him in her arms until he'd settled and then place him into his cot once he was in fairly deep sleep. As a result, he was waking often in the night, needing to be rocked again. He regularly woke up at 5 a.m., and at that time in the morning it was impossible to get him to resettle.

The solution

In order for Morton to establish a pattern of consistent daytime naps and peaceful night-time sleep, he needed to:

1. learn how to fall asleep independently and happily at the beginning of the night
2. apply his night-time sleep skills to his daytime naps.

The plan

- Follow a highly consistent bedtime routine, comprising a series of familiar steps leading up to bedtime. In time, these steps will ensure that Morton feels not only safe and secure, but sleepy, too.
- Start the routine at around 6 p.m., unless Morton has inadvertently fallen asleep at teatime, in which case he should be allowed to sleep for no more than 40 minutes and the bedtime routine should begin two and a half hours later. For instance, if Morton slept between 4.30 and 5 p.m., the routine should start at 7.30 p.m.
- After his bath, offer him milk as usual in his room, but keep a soft light on and discourage him from falling asleep during the feed.
- While one of you is settling Morton, the other should put Iris to bed. Warn her that she might hear her baby brother crying, but to be reassured that Mummy or Daddy is with him, teaching him how to sleep and that he is not alone.
- After Morton's milk, introduce him to a goodnight story book in his room before placing him in his cot. This will help to provide a new sleep trigger for him instead of the ritual of being rocked or fed to sleep. The book needs to be the same one each night until his settling skills are very strong.
- When the story is over, Morton needs to go in his cot while wide awake.

Nights 1 and 2

Lean over the cot and cuddle/stroke/pat Morton until he begins to settle. As he eventually calms down, withdraw the amount of your contact until just your hand is gently resting on him or holding his hand.

If Morton struggles to get up, kneel next to him with your arms around him, but do not lift him out of the cot. Speak softly, using repetitive phrases or hum to him. As he eventually becomes sleepy, lie him down and then, if necessary, lean right over into the cot and cuddle him. Do not pick him up and cuddle him to sleep. It is very important for Morton to know that he is in his cot as he falls asleep. Throughout his crying and protest at the change, maintain a calm and loving demeanour.

From night 1, both of you should go to bed early and be mentally prepared to be up in the night. Morton might wake up more often than ever at first, due to his feelings of insecurity at the changes in his settling routine. When he wakes in the night, leave him to see if he can resettle by himself. If his crying becomes more persistent, however, go to him and settle him as you did at the beginning of the evening, without getting him out of his cot.

Nights 3 and 4
- Maintain the new settling measures that you have introduced on the previous two nights, but begin to move away from him slightly. Cut down on eye contact and avoid touching him after your initial kiss goodnight and tuck-in.

Nights 5 and 6
- After placing him into his cot, quietly potter around his room. You can return to him to pat, reassure and lay him back down whenever he needs you to.

Night 7
- Say goodnight to Morton in your usual way, stay for a moment or two and then quietly leave. If he calls out or cries, go back to him, stroke his back or tummy for a moment, then go through the withdrawal stages (taking about five minutes over this) and then leave again.
- If necessary, keep on returning to him and do not allow him to become distressed at any stage. Most important, however, is that, however long it takes Morton to settle, you should not be in the room with him as he falls asleep.
- Treat any waking before 7 a.m. as a night waking. After 7 a.m., you should open the curtains in Morton's room and welcome him to the day, with as much cheerfulness as you can muster!

Daytime
- For the first week of the sleep plan, while Morton is learning how to settle to sleep at night, help him go to sleep at regular times in the day, so that his body gets into the rhythm of napping. At first you can help him to go to sleep by taking him for a walk in the pram or taking him out in the car.
- Daytime sleep skills tend to be more fragile than night-time ones, so you can expect Morton to require extra help to wind down for his naps. What is very important is that he is well rested during the day, as overtiredness will impact on the progress you are making in establishing his night-time settling skills.
- Offer two daytime naps, with one of these being shorter than the other. It doesn't matter which one that is. Watch out for signs that

Morton is becoming tired during the day. These include yawning, eye rubbing, becoming short-tempered or crying. Before these signs go on for any length of time and he becomes overtired, help put him to sleep in whatever way you can.

- Timing of the naps should be scheduled for around 10 a.m. and 3.p.m. (or one hour either side of these times) but be flexible about this. It is more important to watch for Morton's sleepy signs.
- If he wakes up from his nap after less than 45 minutes and still appears to be sleepy, try to resettle him for up to 20 minutes. If at the end of this time he shows no signs of going back to sleep, you should allow him to get up.
- After one or two weeks of implementing the sleep plan at night, you need to encourage Morton to apply the skills that he has learned to his daytime naps. Instead of taking him out in his pram or the car for his naps, settle him at home. By now he should have established regular times and durations for his naps, so you will have a better idea of when to settle him.
- Follow a mini bedtime routine when settling him down during the day. Go to his bedroom, close the curtains and change his nappy if necessary. Remove his outer clothing and put him into his night-time sleeping bag. Read his usual bedtime storybook and after this place him into his cot while he is awake. Leave him to settle alone. If he cries, return to him every five minutes or so to reassure him, but do not stay with him. Eventually, he will settle to sleep without you, but this might take some time.
- If Morton sleeps for longer than usual, don't worry. There is no need to wake him up unless it gets to 4 p.m., after which time his late napping might interfere with his usual bedtime.
- Morton is not yet ready to have just one long nap in the day, but he soon will be. You need to follow his lead on this.

The outcome

It took around two weeks for Morton's sleep difficulties to completely resolve into a pattern of good night-time sleep and daytime napping, but there were some great improvements from the very moment his parents started the plan.

Once his problems had resolved, the change in him was remarkable. He was better tempered and less clingy to his mother. The whole family benefited from Morton's improved sleep skills: Iris found that her parents were less tired and they had more time for her on her own.

His parents hadn't realized just how exhausted they had become through constantly trying to comfort Morton, both during the night and in the daytime, too. They were at last getting time to catch up on their own sleep.

The family liked the idea of tackling Morton's sleep troubles in two stages. They felt it was a gentle and sensible approach. Given that they had faith in the plan and were motivated to change, they had very good results.

Top tips: daytime naps, six to 12 months

- Take note of the times that your baby appears to be sleepy during the day and follow her lead.
- Encourage your baby to establish good independent sleep skills at night, which can then be transferred to daytime.
- Just as at bedtime, allow your baby to self-settle.
- Follow a mini bedtime routine before settling your baby in her cot during the day, including keeping the room as dark as possible.
- If she wakes after a short time, allow her the opportunity to self-settle if she is just 'fussing'. Help her to resettle by patting and so on only if she really needs you to.
- Recognize that your baby is an individual and may not fit the textbook norm of daytime sleep patterns set out for babies of her age.
- Don't become a prisoner in your home. Sleep taken when out and about in the pram or car can be just as restorative as sleep taken in the cot.
- Be flexible: your baby's daytime sleep needs will change as she grows.
- Do not rush to get your baby up if she wakes after a short nap. If you allow her time to resettle, she may sleep for longer and wake up better rested.

The older baby who will sleep only in your bed

There are two main reasons why babies of six to 12 months old want to sleep in bed with their parents:

1. They fall asleep in your bed at the beginning of the night.
2. They are used to the ritual of being brought into your bed at some point during the night or early morning.

It might at times appear that your baby hates or fears her cot. Babies are very good at letting us know when they are unhappy about something, and if your baby cries each time she is in her cot, you cannot be blamed for thinking that there is something the matter *with the cot*. It is very rarely the case that the cot is wrong, however. What babies do not like is the *unfamiliar*.

Look at this scenario:

> You follow a perfect bedtime routine and then give your baby her bedtime feed cuddled up on your bed. She either falls asleep on her milk or you hold her in your arms before she snuggles down and goes to sleep. You gently place her into her cot and tiptoe out of the room. It may be shortly afterwards or several hours later that she wakes up with an outraged and upset cry. You hurry back to her and comfortingly scoop her up into your arms. You either feed her or cuddle her again in your bed until she is soothed back to sleep. You may put her back into her cot if it is still early, or, if it is nearly morning, she will stay in the bed with you. Even if you have put her back into her cot, it is really only a matter of time before she wakes again and you bring her into the bed with you. She then sleeps peacefully until morning, perhaps with the odd tiny feed or cuddle when she stirs.

Does that sound familiar? How about this other scenario?

> Your baby always goes to sleep beautifully in her cot at the beginning of the night. She has a good bedtime routine followed by a story and a milk feed in her room. She goes into her cot either asleep or even awake sometimes, and then settles with minimal, if any crying. Despite this, she still wakes up in the night. By this time you are very tired, and you bring her into bed with you, where she settles immediately and sleeps well for the remainder of the night. Occasionally, you have resolved to keep her in her cot for

the night, but each time you try, her crying is upset to the point of hysteria.

In the first scenario, it is clear that the baby is never aware of being put into her cot. Each time she wakes, she panics to find herself in an unfamiliar place. Her parents' response is to remove her immediately and to take her to their bed (a place that feels safe and familiar). Unwittingly, by doing this, the baby's feeling that the cot is the wrong place for her to be in is being reinforced.

In the second scenario, the baby is happy to settle into her cot, but has become accustomed to the *ritual* of transferring to her parents' bed. Babies and children get hooked on to rituals very early in life, and these familiar, predictable behaviour patterns are hugely important to them. When you try to change a ritual (in particular, a night-time ritual), the protest from your baby will be massive.

When you do decide to alter your baby's night-time rituals, it is important to realize that this protest is not an expression of fear or abandonment. Neither is it anything to do with fear of her cot.

It is easy to see why this extreme protest may seem like fear of the cot. Before you move her to a bed or travel cot or before you rush out and spend money on a set of new bedding, consider what the benefits will be of gently teaching her to accept the cot she has now as a safe and permanent sleeping place.

> At the age of six months, we moved William into his own room, but from the start he seemed to hate his cot. I was upset, as I'd put lots of thought into making his room and bed lovely and welcoming. We'd splashed out on a gorgeous cot, which would convert to a bed when he was bigger. It seemed like he was never going to be happy sleeping there, though.
>
> At the beginning of the night, he would fall asleep during his last breast feed, which I gave in my bedroom. The reason

for this was that I liked to relax and watch TV during this feed. It was a good way for both of us to unwind and I felt that this feed was very unrushed and relaxed. I'm sure that some of the programme theme tunes acted as 'lullabies' for William, too!

Once he fell asleep, I would always place him into his cot. The problems began sometime after midnight, when he would wake up and I couldn't resettle him in his cot. I knew that he wasn't hungry, as he was feeding well in the day, and a breast feed didn't settle him anyway. As he got older, he used to actually point to his doorway, as if he was telling me that he wanted to come to my bed. As soon as I walked out of his room with him, he would clearly relax in my arms and he fell asleep virtually the moment he came into my bed.

It became a routine that my husband would silently get up and almost sleepwalk to our bed, where he would spend the rest of the night.

After taking advice, we decided to teach William that his cot was a safe and permanent sleeping place. We began by giving his bedtime feed in his room, rather than in ours. After this, I would put him into his cot while he was still awake. He protested for a couple of nights but was tired and settled after half an hour or so. During the night, I would go to him, feed him very briefly and then place him back into his cot before he fell asleep. One of us would stay beside him, to comfort him as he got used to sleeping in what was actually a new place for him.

It was a difficult but ultimately rewarding experience, as within a week, William had stopped waking up during the night. We had our bed to ourselves, and William was much happier. This was due, I'm sure, to the improvement in the quality of his sleep.

Neither of us had realized just how tired we had become, having our baby in bed with us each night. It is only now that we feel rested enough to really enjoy William's babyhood.

> **Insight**
> - Your baby wants to sleep all night in her cot. She demands to come into your bed because she is accustomed to the ritual.
> - Her coming into your bed is habitual and not an emotional plea for your attention.

Dropping night breast feeds

By the time your baby reaches the age of six months, provided that she is healthy, gaining weight nicely and has started solid food, it is very possible that she no longer requires a night feed for nutritional reasons. Lots of babies will drop night feeds without help once they reach a certain weight and when their sleep skills have matured. For many babies, however, night feeds will continue long after they are still needed. The reasons for this unnecessary feeding include:

- needing to feed as a sleep prompt
- learned hunger
- habit and ritual.

Many parents choose to continue to breastfeed in the night until their baby is over a year or no longer asks for it. This is absolutely fine, of course, especially if you feel confident about and in control of that decision. It is OK to carry on breast-feeding in the night for as long as you like. It is also OK to stop when you've had enough – especially if the disturbed nights are affecting your mental and/or physical health.

Although breastfeeding at night helps to ensure a healthy milk supply for the following day, by the time your baby is six months old, your supply will be sufficiently established that your body will still make milk for the daytime feeds. Breast milk production is about supply and demand. When the night feeds are dropped, the day feeds will increase and feeding regularly in the day will keep your milk supply up. If you are returning to work and not intending to express milk to leave with a carer, your body will then simply make milk for the times when it is needed – even if that's just for a morning and bedtime feed.

Case study
Twelve-month-old baby girl: dependent on breastfeeding for sleeping

Felicity was the youngest of three girls. Her older sisters, Hannah and Isobel – five and three years old, respectively – shared a bedroom and slept through the night. Felicity had her own little room and cot. As babies, Hannah and Isobel each had had sleep difficulties similar to their baby sister's. Both were breastfed during the night until well after their first birthdays. Their mother Ruth was now at home full time, caring for the family. Their father Mike worked full time.

Felicity had no health problems; she was developing well and had recently started walking.

The problem

Despite Felicity's recent increase in expending energy, she was not sleeping well at all. Typically, she would fall asleep on the breast at the beginning of the night and then wake up to six times a night for short 'top-up' feeds. She was clingy and tired during the day and was taking virtually no solids. Clearly, the reason for her poor daytime appetite was excessive milk intake during the night.

The solution

Felicity needed to drop all of her night breast feeds if she was to learn how to sleep through the night, and for her daytime appetite to improve. Whereas once, breastfeeding had been a lovely way of settling Felicity to sleep at night, it had now become the very reason for her wakefulness.

The plan

Stage 1

Ruth needs to work to break the breast–sleep connection. The process will be prolonged if Mike is to take over the night care, as Felicity will still expect a breast feed each time her mother tries to settle her. Mike can support Ruth by taking over the girls' care in the morning, to give Ruth a much-needed sleep in the morning. For this reason, the sleep plan should be started on a Friday night.

- Avoid allowing Felicity any daytime sleep after 3 p.m.
- Offer a carbohydrate-rich supper and plenty of fluids (breast or water) during the day. As her daytime appetite is small, and she can easily become overwhelmed with food, it is best to give tiny portions and then offer second helpings, rather than overwhelm her with a large dish of food.
- Develop a highly repetitive and consistent bedtime routine. Always give Felicity a bath and, after this, go directly to her room to settle her to sleep. Aim to have her in her cot by 7.30 p.m.
- Mike is to put Hannah and Isobel to bed, while Ruth concentrates on Felicity.
- Breastfeed her on a chair in her own bedroom, with the light kept on, and do not allow her to fall asleep at the breast. It is most important that you are sitting up when you feed her. If you lie down, you are giving Felicity the message that you will be staying with her for the night.
- After the feed, cuddle up with Felicity and together look at a familiar picture book – the same one each night. If she refuses this, remain calm and just show her the book cover before moving on to the next stage.
- Start a 'kiss goodnight' ritual prior to putting Felicity into her cot awake.
- When/if she cries, give her as much physical contact as she needs to help her to feel safe. You can stroke and pat her and even lean right into her cot and put yourself close beside her. You must not, however, lift her out of the cot. If you do this, Felicity will expect another breast feed, and it will be difficult for you to refuse. If she goes to sleep aware that she is in her own cot, even if she has cried and even if you have been beside her, that is marvellous progress and she is well on the way to sleeping through the night. As she is crying, remind yourself that Felicity is neither hungry nor frightened. She is tired and frustrated, because she wants to sleep and doesn't have the skills yet. Stay positive as this is what you are teaching her now.
- As she begins to sleep, withdraw the amount of physical contact, so that you are just quietly sitting by her cot.
- When she is fully asleep, you need to leave and go to bed early yourself.
- When Felicity first wakes up during the night, go to her and breastfeed her in her room. After the feed, you should place her back in her cot while she is still awake.

- Expect some more crying, but try to demonstrate a calm and positive manner. Settle her as you have done earlier in the evening and do not be disheartened, as Felicity will very soon learn to be content in her own cot.
- Here is a suggested regime for how to eventually withdraw. Each step should last for as many nights as you feel comfortable with. After a brief breast feed:
  - **Step 1** Stroke Felicity's back or lean right over into the cot and cuddle her. You must not rock or feed her to sleep. She needs to know where she is.
  - **Step 2** Just sit with a hand on her back. If she wants you to stroke her, do so but cut down on the duration. As she enters sleep, do not be touching her at all.
  - **Step 3** Sit beside the cot and just touch Felicity's hand.
  - **Step 4** Move yourself away from her slightly. Cut down on eye contact and avoid touching her as she goes off to sleep.
  - **Step 5** After Felicity's feed, place her in her cot and then leave. You may need to pop back in a few times to reassure her as she settles.
- It is clear that Felicity needs to have milk during the night for the following reasons:
  - learned hunger
  - sleep prompt.
- By cutting the duration of the feeds and not allowing her to fall asleep on the breast, you are now directly addressing both reasons for her unnecessary night feeding.
- Each time she wakes up, go through the same routine and treat anything before 6.30 a.m. as a night waking.
- Any time after 6.30 a.m., first open the bedroom curtains and then welcome Felicity to the day. After this, you can give her her morning breast feed, but do not let her go back to sleep!
- Stage 1 should take between one and two weeks to complete. You should be firm and consistent but not rush Felicity too much and only move on to stage 2 when you are both feeling comfortable.

Stage 2
Mike can help during the night now. Once again, commence this on a Friday night.

- Ruth should continue to settle Felicity in the same way at the beginning of the night. The bedtime (7.30 p.m.) feed should be maintained but Felicity should not have another breast feed until she gets up for the day.

- Each time she wakes up in the night, leave her for a moment to see if she can settle herself. If her crying becomes urgent or distressed, Ruth should go to her and reassure her. If necessary, you can stay with her, but she must remain in her cot.
- After a very few times settling without a feed, Felicity will soon lose her milk/sleep association. She has been very well prepared during the previous stage on how to fall asleep without the breast in her mouth.
- Once Felicity is no longer expecting a breast feed during the night, you can cut down on the length of time you spend comforting her in her cot, so that she is able to resettle without help each time she rouses during the night. By this time, either one of you can go to her to settle her during the night.

The outcome

Felicity really struggled at first, breaking her normal settling pattern. She did not want the breast feed to stop before she had gone to sleep, and she let her mother know how unhappy she was.

This was very hard for Ruth, whose natural mothering style was to feed her baby on demand. She realized, however, that to meet the challenge of bringing up three very little girls, she needed her baby and herself to be well rested. She stuck with it, and even in the first week, while she was still breastfeeding at night, she saw some very positive changes.

Felicity went from feeding six times a night to just once or twice.

Over the next few days, Felicity began to eat more during the day and actually seemed to enjoy her food, too.

By the second week, her parents were feeling confident about dropping the night breast feeds altogether. There were a few tears but no real distress, as they had equipped Felicity with the skills to sleep without the breast. Before the two weeks were up, she was sleeping all night in her cot.

Conclusion

By understanding the reason for Felicity's frequent night waking and excessive night feeding, the family were able to solve her sleep difficulties in a sensitive and gentle way. They particularly liked being able to tackle the problem in stages and having permission to take things at their own and Felicity's pace. Sleep problems are always more successfully treated if the family is able to accept and understand the reasons for the offered solution.

Insight

Breast milk is very low in iron, although the iron present is much easier to absorb than that in cows' milk. Full-term babies are born with their own in-built stock of iron which lasts them for the first four to six months. After this time, they need to get this essential nutrient from other sources.

There is absolutely no question at all that breast milk is the perfect food for babies up to the age of six months. They require nothing more than this. After six months, breast milk is still a highly nutritious and fabulous drink; however, it is no longer a complete food. Your baby will need to have other food, too.

Night breastfeeding to excess can sometimes lead to a baby not eating other essential food during the daytime. In some cases, babies can run the risk of developing iron deficiency: anaemia.

If your baby has a tiny appetite, you need to watch out that she is not over-breastfeeding and offer her food that is rich in both iron and vitamin C (which is needed to absorb the iron that she eats).

Symptoms of anaemia are:

- pale skin
- tiredness
- fast heartbeat – but remember that a normal baby's pulse is faster than yours
- irritability
- reduced appetite
- brittle nails
- sore or swollen tongue.

A baby with mild or developing anaemia may not show these (rather vague) symptoms. If you are concerned about your baby's eating, and she shows any of the above signs, you should seek advice from your GP, paediatrician or health visitor.

Iron-rich food for breastfed babies

- leafy dark green vegetables – especially watercress
- lean meat – including chicken and fish
- pulses
- well-cooked egg yolk
- fortified breakfast cereals
- follow-on formula, either given as an additional drink or mixed with food

As well as being not always necessary nutritionally, very frequent or constant night breastfeeding can sometimes prevent babies developing essential self-settling skills and can lead to daytime sleep problems, too. All in all, you can run the risk of your baby becoming overtired and overdependent on you for all of their sleep needs. You may find yourself becoming extremely tired and run down and lacking the energy to cope with her increased mobility and need for activity and stimulation. You may also worry particularly about your baby's ability to settle if you are preparing to return to work. You should not feel guilty if you want to drop the night feeds now.

It is a shame, when you have done such a great job in breast-feeding, to find yourself confronted with these difficulties. However, you need to be clear in your own mind that, even if your baby does have a sleep problem related to breastfeeding, you have given her the best. Nothing can take away the early benefits, both nutritional and emotional, that you have given to her by feeding her yourself.

Top tips: dropping night breast feeds

- Establish a familiar bedtime routine.
- Do not allow your baby to fall asleep on the breast at the start of the night.

- Introduce a song or story after the feed and before she goes into her cot. This will break the milk/sleep association.
- Keep night feeds very short, and always place her back in her cot while she is awake. This will further help to break the milk/sleep association.
- After a few nights of this, drop the night breast feeds all at once and, if necessary, comfort your baby in the cot.
- It is less confusing for your baby and perfectly safe at this age if, after shortening the duration of the feeds, you stop them altogether.
- You may need to express some milk, for your own comfort, but your body will soon adjust.
- Try not to confuse your baby by withholding or restricting night feeds and then giving a big, sleepy feed at dawn. Your baby can't tell the time yet, and as far as she is concerned, this is a night feed.

Remember, then, that while breastfeeding your baby at night when she is very little and growing rapidly is one of the best things that you can do for her, after about six months old, if she is asking for very frequent night breast feeds, these may no longer be beneficial and can sometimes be detrimental to her daytime appetite and nap routine.

Dropping night bottle feeds

As with night breast feeds, night formula feeds are often unnecessary once a baby gets to six months old and is on solid food. The ritual of feeding at night can become a habit that is very difficult to break. During the middle of the night, your older baby's body needs to rest. Keeping her body working by having her digest formula feeds is not conducive to enjoying a good night's sleep.

Not only is prolonged bottle feeding at night unnecessary and bad for your baby's digestion, it is also bad for her growing teeth. Having milk pooling in your baby's mouth can lead to tooth decay. As soon as her first tooth arrives, you need to start a gentle teeth cleaning ritual after her bedtime bottle. This also gives you the opportunity to wake her and read a little story before settling her in her cot while she is awake.

Another very important consideration is the safety aspect of giving night feeds. This is particularly relevant for babies who self-feed in the cot during the night. It is terribly important to discourage this kind of feeding, due to the risk of choking and/or vomiting.

Five good reasons why you should not allow your older baby to bottle feed to sleep

1 She may learn to associate sleep with feeding and may only be able to fall asleep while taking a bottle.
2 This may lead to unnecessary feeding at night, which will impair her appetite for the food which she needs during the day.
3 Feeding during the night overworks your baby's digestive system.
4 Night bottle feeds are bad for her developing teeth and may cause tooth decay.
5 There is a risk of choking if you leave your baby to self-feed during the night.

Case study
Eleven-month-old baby boy: waking for night bottle feeds
Billy was the second and had older sister Melissa, who was three years old and had no problems with her sleep. Billy slept in a cot in his own room.

Billy was born by emergency Caesarean section at 38 weeks but was healthy and had had an uneventful infancy. After ten weeks of being breastfed, he had moved on to formula feeds with no problems. His weight gain and development were both excellent. His mother said his only real difficulty was that he suffered a lot from 'trapped wind', particularly during the night.

The problem
Although Billy had a great bedtime routine, he would fall asleep every night in his cot, with his mum holding his bottle and him feeding to

sleep. He normally settled very quickly like this, but once he had gone to sleep, he would stir once or twice before his parents went to bed and would need to be fed back to sleep with a little more milk. This was always given to him in his cot.

At around 2 a.m., he would wake up fully and take a full 8-oz (235-ml) bottle. Prior to this, however, he would stir frequently and need to have his back stroked, or be helped to sit up until he passed wind.

Occasionally, Billy would take another big bottle of milk at around 5 a.m. before resettling and sleeping until morning.

It was clear that Billy was feeding as frequently as a much younger baby. His night-time milk drinking was both preventing him from enjoying sustained sleep and interfering with his appetite for solid food during the day.

The solution

Billy is easily capable of sleeping through the night, and for him to do this, he needs to:

- fall asleep at the beginning of the night after and not during his night bottle
- gently drop all of his night feeds. As he is so accustomed to taking large quantities of milk at night, the best way for him to achieve this is by having the feeds gradually diluted.

The plan

Nights 1 and 2

- Continue to follow a highly ritualized but very simple bed-time routine, using key phrases/songs/actions etc. This will help Billy to feel safe and sleepy, too.
- After his bath and putting his pyjamas on, you should take him directly to his room and sit him on your knee for his bottle of milk.
- When he has had enough milk, put the bottle out of sight. After this, you should sit with him and spend a little time looking at a picture book and 'winding' him. Use the same book each night until his sleep problems have resolved. Billy will be very restless and unwilling to look at the book at first, so don't feel that you must read to him for long.
- After looking at the book, pick him up and develop a goodnight ritual of turning the lights down and closing the curtains, etc. After this, say goodnight in your usual way, and place him in his cot while he is still awake.

- Billy will protest at being placed in his cot without his bottle. If necessary, you can stay beside him but not lift him out of his cot. To make things easier for him, one of you can sit beside the cot with your arms around him. In time, his crying will subside and he will lie down. Praise him warmly as he does this.
- To cope with the crying, remind yourselves that he is neither hungry nor frightened. He is tired and frustrated, and he wants to sleep. You should be positive, as this is what you are teaching him now. Spend as much time as you need to with him and do not be disheartened; it is worth investing this time and effort. Settle him this way for the first two nights of the sleep programme.
- Billy will only sleep through the night when he is able to settle to sleep without either of you in the room with him, so you need to eventually withdraw as he goes to sleep.

Nights 3 and 4

- By now, Billy will be happier with the new routine and about going in his cot without his milk. He should lie down by himself after a brief cuddle, but if he doesn't do this, you should encourage (but not force) him to lie down. You need to sit quietly beside him but reduce eye contact with him. If he wants you to stroke him, you can do so but you should cut down on the duration. As he enters sleep, you should not be touching him at all.

Nights 5 and 6

- Try pottering around the room, returning to Billy every now and then if he needs you to. It is still all right to be next to him as he goes to sleep.

Night 7

- Say goodnight in your usual way, potter around for a moment or two and then leave. If Billy calls out or cries, you can go back to him, stroke his back for a minute, then leave again. If his crying is any more than a 'complaint' or 'grumble', you can keep on returning to him every five minutes or so, but you are not to go in if his cries are minor.
- If he wakes up any time after midnight, you should lift him from his cot and offer him a bottle of milk. This milk should be normal volume but diluted as follows:
  - Nights 1 and 2   ¾ strength
  - Nights 3 and 4   ½ strength
  - Nights 5 and 6   ¼ strength
  - Night 7 onwards Nothing, unless he is unwell and then just water.

- It is important that, after his milk, you remove the bottle while he is still awake and that he is awake when you put him back in his cot.
- If necessary, you can sit beside him if you had done so at the beginning of the night.
- This diluted milk can be given more than once during the night if needed.
- If he is still waking up after you have weaned him off the milk, you can go to him but do not lift him out of his cot. Reassure him and then leave him to go off to sleep alone.
- Billy should be offered a morning bottle (any time after 6 a.m.) downstairs – not in the bedroom, and not in his cot.
- It is vital that, during the sleep training, you demonstrate a calm, confident and resolute attitude.

The outcome

Billy had already got a great bedtime routine and was not in the habit of getting into his parents' bed during the night. He was having one good long nap during the day, so he was sleepy but not overtired at bedtime. Because his parents were already doing so much right, solving Billy's sleep problem was not as difficult as they thought it might be.

The worst night was the first one. Billy was desperately upset that his normal settling routine had changed, and it took him almost two hours of on-and-off crying before his sobs eventually gave way to sleep.

His mum, in particular, found this very hard. The fact that she was sitting beside him, however, helped her to cope. She felt that not only was she supporting him, but she was going through the battle with him, too.

His dad knew this was going to be hard for her, and he waited outside the room, murmuring his support and encouragement. It helped her, knowing that she was not facing this alone.

On the first night, once he had gone to sleep, Billy did not wake as usual, early in the evening. His first wake-up was for his 2 a.m. feed.

He accepted his diluted bottle but cried again for around half an hour when he was placed back in his cot while still awake and without the teat in his mouth. He then slept on until 6.30 a.m.

Over the following nights, his parents continued to put him down awake and to dilute the night bottle. Each night they found that Billy coped better than on the previous one.

Billy stopped waking for his night feeds before he even got on to quarter-strength milk. For two or three weeks, however, he fell into a pattern of waking at the very early time of 5.30 a.m. His parents decided to give a drink of water only at this time, and stick with going in and out of his room every five minutes. Within a month, Billy was sleeping through until the household got up, at 7 a.m.

Each morning, his big sister Melissa was given a sticker on her pyjamas for staying in her bed when she was woken up by Billy. This helped her to feel included in the plan and to see it as a positive thing. It also gave her parents the opportunity to recognize and praise her own good sleep behaviour.

Conclusion

Billy's sleep problem and its resolution show once again how, once you have established the reason for a baby's waking, you can solve it without the unnecessary trauma of simply leaving her to cry it out.

Ten things to remember

1. Babies of six months or more rarely need a night feed.
2. Feeding an older baby during the night can interfere with daytime appetite.
3. Older babies need to slow down and rest at night – and this includes their digestive system.
4. A milk/sleep dependence is responsible for lots of babies' sleep problems.
5. Watch out – babies of over six months are actively looking for rituals (such as night feeds or transfers to Mum and Dad's bed!).
6. How you settle your baby to sleep at the start of the night is more important than ever with an older baby. Secure independence is the key.
7. Teach your baby to recognize her cot as a safe and lovely place to be.
8. As your baby becomes more mobile, avoid wrestling matches in the cot. Stay calm and gentle. She will settle down eventually.
9. Six months can be a difficult age for sleep – with teething, introduction of solids and moving to a mature sleep cycle patterns. Be prepared for a challenge.
10. Bear in mind that, between six months and a year, a baby is likely to go through a period of separation anxiety.

5

Sleep advice for one- to two-year-olds

This is a truly magical age. Your baby is growing fast and is enchanting you with his funny expressions and lovely perspective on the world. He is becoming more independent and exploring all around himself. He is toddling, tumbling over, emptying cupboards and getting into mischief. You may breathe a sigh of relief that all of those early feeding and teething worries have been resolved, your confidence as a parent has grown, and even if you do make mistakes, your baby is a lot more robust.

In the second year of life, when your baby is more active than ever, his sleep requirement remains at around 12–14 hours in a 24-hour period. He may, however, drop one of his daytime naps and instead take just one long one in the middle of the day. It is not at all uncommon for babies, especially when they are approaching their second year, to refuse to take a nap altogether. Sometimes babies who have previously been great night-time sleepers will begin to encounter problems at bedtime, too.

Suddenly refusing to go to bed

If you find that at this age your baby protests about going to bed, wakes early in the morning and refuses his nap, it is most likely because he loves life so much that he doesn't want to switch off and miss anything.

Of course, sleep is still absolutely vital for his health, growth and development, and despite his objections, you need to help him to settle down and have both a decent nap and a good night's sleep.

At this age, when your baby's imagination is developing and he begins to worry about scary things, it is more important than ever that you ensure that he has a good bedtime routine. The reassurance of the familiar, repetitive run-up to bedtime will keep him feeling safe and secure. When a baby falls asleep feeling calm, safe and happy, he is more likely to sleep through the night.

When Barnaby got to 18 months, he started to protest when I put him to bed for both his daytime nap and at night. Before this, he had always loved his cot, and we hadn't had any problems settling him at all. I was upset, because I knew he needed to sleep, and once I had managed to get him to settle, he slept really deeply.

He was using up loads of energy during the day, was eating well and was not poorly, so I couldn't understand what the problem was.

We spent a few nights bringing Barnaby back downstairs when he cried at bedtime and refused his cot. We would allow him to watch TV and play until he fell asleep on the sofa. Once he was fast asleep, we would put him into his cot. He would sleep well until about 5 a.m., which was far earlier than his usual 7 a.m. waking. We knew that he was still tired but there was absolutely nothing that we could do to help him resettle. We ended up getting him up for the day. Even though he had been up so early, he couldn't settle down for his nap. Having said that, he would fall deeply asleep in the car or in his pram, and by teatime, if he had not been out, he would fall asleep in his food!

After talking to other mums at his music group, I found out that some of his friends had done the same kind of thing. One of the mums told me how she managed to tackle the problem with her little girl, and I followed her advice.

We decided that, even if Barnaby protested at bedtime, we would not bring him back downstairs. Instead, one of us would either stay with him or keep going in and out to him, depending on how upset he was, until he settled to sleep. The first few times that we did this it took him ages to settle, but we knew that he needed to fall asleep in his cot rather than downstairs on the sofa. We also knew that we had to break the new ritual of him automatically coming downstairs after his bath. Even though it was hard, it only took him a few nights to start going to sleep in his cot again.

Once we had got the beginning of the night sorted out, the early-morning waking seemed to resolve itself of its own accord. We then needed to tackle his daytime nap. I decided to set aside some time so that I could start a daytime ritual, which included lunch, teeth cleaned, face and hands washed and then his nappy changed. We followed this with a quiet period of reading a story in his room before putting him into his cot. He complained at first, and it took a long time before he settled and slept. During this time, I sat quietly beside him, reading and reassuring him when he needed it. After a week or two (longer than it took for him to learn how to settle again at night) Barnaby began to accept having his daytime nap again. He has been so much more relaxed and cheerful since he has been getting the rest that he needs.

This aversion to sleep is not at all uncommon between 12 and 24 months and beyond. It is important to be aware that it can happen and to take a firm but understanding approach to handling it.

Remember how important it is for your baby, when growing into a toddler, to have as much sleep as possible. Remember, too, that if you begin to allow your baby to delay or lose sleep altogether, it can be difficult to regain his previously good sleep skills. Allowing him to get up and play after his refusal to go to sleep in his cot will only reinforce that behaviour and will very soon become a habit.

Top tips: re-establishing good sleep skills

- Do not allow your baby to over-nap or nap too late in the day.
- Stick to a reassuringly consistent bedtime routine.

- Be prepared for protest, and do not give way by getting him up if he refuses or struggles to settle to sleep.
- Praise him when he is in his cot, in order for him to develop positive associations with bedtime.
- Use simple role-play techniques, using dolls and teddies to demonstrate good sleep behaviour.

The changing face of daytime naps

By the time your baby reaches 18 months, and often before this, he is likely to move from having two or three daytime naps to just one one-and-a-half to two-hour nap in the middle of the day. You need to be prepared for this to happen and to go along with the change. You may notice, first of all, that your baby begins to refuse his morning nap, or to sleep for just a very short period. If he does this, he is telling you that he is ready to move on to one later and longer nap. Don't be concerned: this one nap will be just as good for him, and one special benefit for you is that you will have the opportunity, while he is resting, to catch up on your own jobs or even have a rest yourself.

The transition from two or more naps to just one is not always straightforward. Your baby's sleep needs will change gradually rather than overnight, and you may experience a confusing period when he sometimes wants a morning nap and sometimes doesn't. You may also find that he naps in the morning and then does not want to sleep again until teatime, when it is too late, and may interfere with his usual bedtime. It may be helpful for you to keep a sleep diary of his naps, including the following information: when he appears to be tired; when you put him to bed; whether he cries and, if so, for how long; how long it takes for him to go to sleep; and how long he sleeps. This will give you helpful insight into when best to schedule his nap(s). Don't worry if he is not doing the same as his peers or if he doesn't fit the textbook standard. He is an individual, and all babies progress at different rates.

My baby refuses his morning nap. What can I do?

- Watch out for signs that your baby is getting tired and then put him to sleep. Try to be flexible when he is over one year and be aware that his sleep needs may be changing.
- Be aware that he may be moving towards a more mature napping pattern of a long sleep in the middle of the day.
- Do not force him to sleep or allow him to cry alone in his room if he is simply not tired. He may develop negative feelings about his cot, and this could have a detrimental effect on his night-time sleep.
- Keep a sleep diary. This will help you to see how his natural sleep tendency is emerging. You can then work with this, rather than forcing your baby into a napping routine which is no longer appropriate for his needs.

But when am I going to feed him?

It can cause logistical difficulties when your baby wants to nap just when you usually give him his lunch. If this is the case, you have two options:

1. Give him a late-morning substantial snack and then follow this by a later lunch when he wakes after his nap.
2. Give him an earlier lunch, and then, mid-afternoon, offer a snack which will keep him going until his usual tea or supper time.

Remember that, for your baby to sleep well, he needs to be well fed but his tummy should not be overfull. By the time your baby is one year old, his milk requirement will have dropped to just one pint (560 ml) a day. This is usually taken as a large morning and bedtime feed (bottle or breast), with the shortfall being made up by adding milk to breakfast cereal or other food. If your baby has been used to having a lunchtime feed in addition to this and he is now sleeping when this feed is due, it is perfectly all right to give it either before he goes to sleep or later, when he wakes up.

My baby refuses his afternoon nap, but then falls asleep at teatime. What can I do?

- Gradually cut the duration of, and then drop, the morning nap.
- Bring the afternoon nap forward and merge the two naps into one long one in the middle of the day.
- Do not try to force him to sleep at his usual time if he is simply not tired.
- Embrace his changing sleep needs, and keep a sleep diary. This will help you feel in control and in tune with his needs.
- Offer him an afternoon snack to boost his blood sugar and keep him going.
- If you absolutely cannot avoid him falling asleep, limit the nap to 20 minutes, and be prepared to push bedtime a little bit later.
- If and when he does take a single nap in the middle of the day, you may need to bring his bedtime forward.

There is no hard-and-fast rule as to how long the gap should be between your baby waking up from his last daytime nap and the time you put him to bed. In babies of this age, it tends to be about three to four hours, but your baby might be different. *You know your baby best.* If you read your baby's body language, as only you can do, you will find the right bedtime for him.

The great dummy debate

Many parents encourage their babies to have a dummy for the first six months, as, a few years ago, some research suggested that dummy use offered protection against cot death. Dummies have always been the subject of often heated debate. There is no doubt that they do, in some circumstances, have their advantages.

Six dummy plus-points

In the first six months, dummy use may:

- help reduce the risk of cot death in the early weeks and months
- help ease the symptoms of colic and reflux
- help a 'sucky' baby to drop unnecessary feeds
- provide comfort during teething
- help premature, tube-fed babies to establish feeding from the breast or bottle
- help induce sleep through the rhythmic and natural sucking process.

After the age of six months, however, dummy use can be problematic and can even end up working against you rather than to your advantage. This is particularly the case if your baby becomes overdependent on his dummy and is only able to fall asleep while sucking.

When your baby falls asleep, his dummy is likely to fall out of his mouth. The nature of sleep is such that frequent waking up due to the sleep cycles means that he may need his dummy replacing several times.

During the first year or two of your baby's life, when he is teething or has a cold, his tiny nasal passages will become easily blocked. When this happens, he will struggle to breathe through his nose. This is especially difficult for him when he is lying flat in his cot.

In order to keep his dummy in place, he needs to be able to breathe freely through his nose; otherwise his dummy will fall out. For a baby who is only able to sleep with a dummy in situ, this can cause real problems.

If your baby is waking during the night due to problems with his dummy, you have two choices:

1. Get rid of the dummy altogether.
2. Teach him how to manage his dummy independently.

Case study

Fourteen-month-old baby girl: disrupted sleep because of over-dependence on her dummy

Poppy was a lively toddler who was developing beautifully despite having been born two months prematurely. She had been introduced to a dummy at an early age, in an attempt to ease the symptoms of reflux.

As all babies are, Poppy was very precious indeed to her parents. Poppy's mother was early into her pregnancy with their second child and was extremely tired as a result.

The problem

Poppy had a great bedtime routine and settled independently into her cot with her dummy and 'blanky' (comfort blanket).

Despite settling all by herself, she would wake 45 minutes after going to sleep, having invariably lost her dummy, and needing one of her parents to find it for her and help her to resettle. She would subsequently wake up and need help with settling up to a further four times later in the night. Her parents were afraid to take her dummy away, as they could not face their nights becoming any worse than they already were. They also felt that Poppy was vulnerable still, because of her prematurity, and that that any form of sleep training would be not only detrimental to her but also traumatic for them.

After some discussion, it was clear that Poppy was overdependent on a dummy to help her to sleep. This was particularly problematic when she had a blocked nose due to a cold or a teething episode. When she fell asleep, the dummy fell out of her mouth, and when she woke during the light phase of a sleep cycle, she felt something was missing and couldn't resettle without it. She had also come to expect the ritual of contact with her parents when she woke in the night.

The solution

For Poppy to sleep through the night, she needed to do two things:
- learn how to sleep without her dummy
- stay in her cot and overcome her expectation of cuddles and contact with her parents during the night.

The plan

- Tighten up her bedtime routine, so that it becomes a clear system of little sleep triggers.
- Include familiar phrases and a goodnight story in your routine.

- This routine and the verbal sleep triggers will very soon perform the same soothing function as her dummy – but are better for her and will promote more peaceful sleep.
- Put her to bed with her 'blanky' but without her dummy.
- Learning to sleep without her dummy should be taught at the beginning of the night, and then reinforced when she wakes up during the night and then during the following day.
- As Poppy learns to fall asleep without her dummy, one of you should stay beside her to minimize her stress.
- After two nights, her new bedtime routine will be established and she will have learned how to fall asleep without the dummy in her mouth.
- On the third night, gently withdraw and allow Poppy to fall asleep alone again.
- While working towards this objective, support one another and stay calm and resolved.
- For the first two nights, each time she wakes in the night, she will need to be comforted back to sleep in her cot, with one of you beside her. This is instead of bringing her into your bed.
- She will protest at you breaking the normal ritual, but once she realizes that you have not abandoned her, she will soon adapt to the change.
- From the third night, if she continues to wake up, go to her and reassure her very briefly before leaving her to settle by herself.
- Once the dummy has gone and Poppy has stopped expecting to get out of her cot during the night, it is unlikely that she will wake on subsequent nights.

The outcome

On the first night of Poppy's sleep plan, it took 50 minutes to settle her to sleep. As expected, she cried a lot and spent a long time standing up, rattling the bars of her cot. Even though her parents found this very difficult, they managed to remain calm and resolved. Once she had gone to sleep, she did not call out until 3 a.m. This seven-hour stretch was the longest period that she had slept since her birth! Resettling Poppy at 3 a.m. took over an hour, but her crying was not as distressed as it had been at the beginning of the night. She woke up for the day, happily, at 7.30 a.m.

On the second night it took Poppy 20 minutes to settle alone and without her dummy. Her parents took it in turns to go to her, in order for her to realize she would receive the same calm, consistent response from each of them. At 5 a.m., she briefly stirred and called out, but managed to settle back to sleep before her parents got to her.

Since then, apart from odd periods of illness, Poppy has slept through the night.

Conclusion

Poppy was introduced to a dummy for a very good reason, but by the time she was over a year old, the dummy was hindering her sleep. A gradual and supportive approach was acceptable to her loving parents and the strategy worked effectively for them all.

Of course, there may be reasons why you would prefer your baby to keep his dummy. One advantage that your older baby has is that he can be taught how to manage it himself.

Toby was born with a foot deformity, which means that he needs to have frequent surgical operations. He gets a lot of comfort from his dummy, and we feel that it is right for him to have it for as long as he needs it. We have taught him how replace his own dummy when he loses it in the night, and we honestly have no sleep problems with him now.

How to help your older baby manage his dummy himself at night

- During bath time, play 'race for the dummy' game, where you challenge him to beat you at picking up the dummy first and putting it in his mouth.
- Place plenty of dummies in his cot at night, so that he can find a spare if he loses one.
- If he calls out for you during the night, having lost his dummy, always put it in his hand rather than putting it into his mouth for him.

If you choose to give your baby a dummy, there are some guidelines for its safe and responsible use.

Top tips: dummy safety

- Do not dip your baby's dummy into a sweet solution, as this will cause tooth decay.
- Always use an orthodontic teat, which has less of a tendency to push your baby's teeth forward.
- Make sure that your baby's dummy is scrupulously clean and has no cracks or tears in it.
- Never tie, tape or strap the dummy to keep it in your baby's mouth.
- Allow your baby to have his dummy for sleep time only. Having it during the daytime may impair his speech development.
- With very young babies, do not allow the dummy to replace milk feeds.

If your baby is dependent on a dummy to sleep at night, you may dread him giving it up. Remember, though, that although babies protest noisily and vigorously when presented with change, after this protest, they very quickly accept a new behaviour.

If there is no good reason for your baby to have one, it is best to encourage him to give up the dummy.

Five dummy minus-points

1 There is a link between dummy use and ear infections.
2 Using a dummy during the day may delay your baby's speech development.
3 There may be an increased risk of stomach and other infections.
4 Dentists advise against the use of dummies (and thumb sucking) as these can lead to orthodontic problems in the future.
5 Overdependence on a dummy can impair your baby's ability to sleep through the night.

Babies who have good settling skills but still wake during the night

You have a perfect bedtime routine, your baby naps perfectly, settles to sleep all by himself, does not have a night feed and yet he still wakes during the night. What is going wrong?

Babies of this age wake for a reason. Often, there are physical causes, such as illness or discomfort, but if he is waking consistently in the night, there is a very good chance that it is out of *habit*. And the more that the habit is rewarded, then the more firmly entrenched it becomes.

Ways in which you might unwittingly reward night-time waking and cause it to become a habit include:

- bringing your baby into bed with you during the night or at dawn
- lying beside him or on his bedroom floor during the night
- offering an unnecessary night feed
- allowing him to get up and play or watch a video during the night.

Each of these night-time activities, if repeated more than a handful of times, can quickly turn into rituals – and *babies love ritual*.

You may have noticed that your baby's need to follow a familiar ritual can override any other needs that he might have. This explains why, when your baby wakes up at night, even if he is very tired and wants to go to sleep, and even if he has the skills to do so, his need to go through a familiar ritual of contact with you will compel him to remain awake until that ritual has been fulfilled.

Top tip

- Ask yourself what event is happening to make it worth your baby's while waking up during the night.

Case study
Seventeen-month-old baby boy: good settling skills but still waking up during the night

Amir was a healthy baby, and was eating and developing well. He had walked early and was learning to speak now. He loved his grandmother, who looked after Amir when his parents were working.

The problem
Amir had always been a great sleeper until he suffered from an ear infection a few weeks earlier. At this time, his night-time sleep became disrupted and his parents got into the habit of bringing him into their bed to comfort him when he felt poorly. He was now fully recovered, but still woke up during the night in expectation of the transfer to his parents' bed.

Each time that they tried to leave him in his own cot, he would cry in a very distressed way, and they just didn't have the heart to leave him. As soon as he was lifted from his cot, he smiled, and once he was in their bed, he settled immediately.

His parents were concerned about the disruption of both Amir's sleep and their own. When Amir was in bed with them, he would wriggle all night, kicking off the covers and taking up all the space.

The solution
It was explained that, for Amir to sleep through the night again, he needed to overcome the expectation of the ritual transfer to their bed. His parents were reassured that, because he had previously slept well through the night, he would be able to do it again.

The plan
• Stick to your excellent bedtime routine.
• Put Amir to bed as usual and then go to bed very early yourselves. You need to be mentally prepared to be up in the night, investing time to help Amir to sleep independently again.
• When he wakes up during the night, one of you should go to him immediately and then follow the plan below.

Nights 1 and 2
• Sit quietly beside Amir's bed and do not get into conversation with him. Use the 'broken record' technique, which means repeating the same message over and over – for example, 'Ssh, Amir, it's time for sleep now.'

- Expect a lot of crying, but be assured that Amir is neither frightened nor feeling abandoned, as you are right beside him. His crying is an expression of the frustration he feels because you are not following the usual ritual of letting him get into your bed.
- Eventually, he will have to give in to sleep, even though this may take an hour or longer. There is no upper time limit to how long you should sit with him. Stay with him until he has gone off to sleep if leaving him alone is too difficult at this stage.

Night 3
- Do the same as the previous two nights, but move away slightly from Amir's cot. Cut down on eye contact and physical contact with Amir once he is calm. It is all right to remain beside him as he goes to sleep if you still need to. It is very important, however, that you do not get into a bed next to his cot and sleep the night in his room. If you do that, you will begin another unhelpful night-time expectation and ritual.

Night 4 onwards
- By now, Amir should have stopped expecting to come into your bed during the night, and have started to consider his cot as his own safe and permanent sleeping place.
- Follow your usual bedtime routine, allowing Amir to settle independently in the way that used to be normal for him. When he wakes up in the night, leave him for five minutes to see if he can resettle himself. If his cries are mild and more like little moans and grumbles, you can leave Amir for longer. Provided that you are certain that he is not in an uncomfortable position or feeling unwell, you can leave him for an hour or more to resettle by himself.
- If, however, Amir becomes distressed, go to him and briefly reassure him before leaving again and going in every five minutes for the period when the crying is severe. He is no longer expecting to come to your bed now, and very soon he will be sleeping happily again.
- If at any time you are aware that he is awake but quiet and content, you should not go in to him, even if he is awake for an hour or more.
- Treat any time before 7 a.m. as a night waking and keep him in his cot, even if he is awake. When he wakes up any time after 7 a.m., you can open his curtains to give a clear visual cue that it is now morning and that it is OK to get out of his cot.

- You can now bring him to your bed but do not allow him to go back to sleep there. This is important for you, as you enjoy a family cuddle and you do not want Amir to feel rejected or unloved by your not allowing him in bed with you during the night.

The outcome
It took just four nights for Amir to stop waking during the night. Because he had already established good self-settling skills at bedtime, he was soon able to apply them when he woke up during the night. He was only able to do this, however, when his parents helped him to break out of the ritual of them moving him to their bed.

Conclusion
Even babies with good self-settling skills can fall into patterns of night waking after a period of illness or change. Once you have recognized what it is that is reinforcing the waking, it is possible to take sensitive and effective steps towards resolving the problem.

Early waking

Most babies are naturally early risers. Being up before the milkman is all part and parcel of being a parent of a young child, and to a large extent it is something that you have to accept and go along with. Early waking problems are notoriously difficult to tackle, because sleep becomes much lighter as daytime approaches and when your baby has had a long block of sleep (even if it is not enough) he will find it very difficult to resettle. This is especially true in the one- to two-year age group, when babies are only too aware of the delights of the coming day.

Putting your baby to bed later in the evening rarely makes any difference to the time that he wakes in the morning. This is because, if he is overtired at bedtime, he is likely to have higher levels of cortisol. Cortisol is the hormone that keeps us awake and melatonin is the hormone that puts us to sleep. As morning approaches, cortisol levels rise and melatonin levels drop. If a child (or adult for that matter) falls asleep with high levels of cortisol on board, there is a good chance that the natural junction where melatonin drops and cortisol rises will happen earlier. If anything, putting your child to bed earlier than usual can help him to sleep in later in the morning.

Parents vary in their opinions about what constitutes an acceptable getting-up time for their baby, but generally, any time between 6 a.m. and 8 a.m. can be considered a normal wake-up time for a baby.

When might early waking be a problem?

- If your baby wakes before 6 a.m. and is crying and still looking tired.
- If your baby has a ritual of a dawn waking, followed by a milk feed or transfer to your bed – and then going back to sleep.
- If your baby is tired and grumpy on waking and then takes an early, lengthy nap.

If any of the early-waking situations listed in the box sound familiar to you, it is well worth considering applying some gentle sleep training in the early mornings to extend your baby's sleep. Before you start, though, you need to take an honest look at your baby's overall sleep ability. If early waking is part of a picture of generally poor settling and night waking, you need to address these issues first of all. You will get nowhere with morning sleep training if you do not have good bedtime settling practices.

If your baby's early waking is part of his generally poor sleeping skills, you should concentrate on teaching him to fall asleep independently at the start of the night and on removing any incentives for night-time waking. You should then treat the early waking as if it were a night waking, offering the same consistent response as you did at settling and night-waking times. If you approach it in this way, you have a great chance of successfully stopping the early waking without having to resort to specific measures.

Case study
Twenty-month-old baby boy: waking at 5 a.m. every morning
Jack's parents were expecting their second child in a few weeks' time.

The problem
Jack had always been a fragile sleeper. He was used to having his mother or father beside him as he went to sleep at night, but once he had gone off to sleep, he usually slept through the night until around 7 a.m., when he would get up and start the day. Recently, however, he had been waking up at 5 a.m., full of tears, looking very tired but unable to go back to sleep. His mother and father tried giving him a bottle, bringing him into their bed and even putting a video on in his room.

He was not, however, able to go back to sleep.

Jack was then taking a two-hour nap at around 8 a.m. After this nap, he was happy for the day, but became very tired and grumpy at around 4 p.m. He would either fall asleep at this time and then struggle to get off to sleep at bedtime or his mother would keep him going until bedtime, when he would fall asleep over his night-time bottle.

The solution
It was explained to his parents that, for Jack to sleep longer in the morning, he needed to:
- improve his night-time settling skills, which could then be used to get himself back to sleep when he woke up at dawn
- reschedule his daytime napping to prevent him from being either overtired or not tired enough at bedtime.

The plan
- During the day, limit his two-hour morning nap to one hour. Offer a second nap after his lunch. This nap can last for up to two hours if necessary. This daytime schedule will discourage him from becoming overtired at teatime, and prevent him from falling asleep over his bedtime bottle.
- As his early-morning waking improves, encourage Jack to drop the morning nap all together and just offer him one long sleep over the lunchtime period.

- You already have a good bedtime routine. Stick with it, but make sure that Jack does not fall asleep on his last bottle.
- Before putting him in his cot, introduce a picture book to look at for a few moments before saying goodnight. The book needs to be the same one each night, so that it becomes a sleep signal for him.
- Draw the bedroom curtains and place Jack in his cot while he is still awake.
- Sit beside the cot for a few moments and then start to potter quietly around the room, returning to him from time to time if he needs you to.
- As he becomes tired, extend your pottering, so that you are coming in and out of the room every few minutes. If he cries, you can briefly reassure him, but keep on leaving him and remain calm and cheerful.
- As he goes off to sleep, you should not be in the room with him.
- Treat any time before 7 a.m. as a night waking. If he wakes and cries before this time, go to him, but keep him in his cot, and be prepared to stay with him if he is very upset. Do not offer him a bottle of milk – even if he struggles to go back to sleep.
- It is hard for babies to get back to sleep at dawn, even though they need more sleep, so you need to be very patient.
- If he is still awake and showing no signs of going back to sleep when it gets to 7 a.m., you should open his curtains to show him that it is now day time and say, 'Good morning!' Then you can get him up for the day.
- If he manages to go back to sleep before 7 a.m., you should allow him to sleep on freely and then wake naturally. Once again, you should open the curtains and say, 'Good morning!' before getting him up.
- Once Jack has learned some robust self-settling skills at the beginning of the night and has overcome the expectation that he will be lifted from his cot as soon as he wakes up and cries, he will begin to sleep in for longer.
- The change in his daytime napping schedule will help this process along.

The outcome

Jack struggled at first with going to sleep without having his mother beside him, but after three nights, he began to feel more relaxed and was able to fall asleep quickly and all by himself. It took about a week for the early waking to resolve, but he was soon sleeping from 7.30 p.m. to 7 a.m. and having a one-and-a-half to two-hour nap after lunch.

Conclusion

His parents were surprised when it was suggested to them that, to solve the early waking, they needed to address what was happening at the beginning of the night. They stuck with the plan, however, and were delighted that they had good results so quickly.

Early waking and crying

If your child wakes early, is crying, rubbing his eyes and still looking very tired, it is clear that he needs to sleep on for longer. It is not a good idea to leave him alone for a long period to cry before going in to him, as you will teach him that, in order for the day to begin, he has to cry for you. This is not good start to the day for either him or you. It is better to go to him before he becomes upset and tell him that it is still sleep time. Then either remain beside him or keep popping in and out to him until you reach an acceptable getting-up time. When you reach this time, you should open his curtains (even if it is still dark outside) before getting him out of his cot, just to give him a visual prompt that it is now getting-up time. He will soon come to realize that, when the curtains are closed, it means that it is sleep time. If, at the beginning of the night, you incorporate closing his curtains before he goes into his cot as a part of his settling routine, you will further reinforce this message. These visual cues and routines are very important for babies, who obviously are not yet able to tell the time.

Early waking and *not* crying

If a baby has had over ten hours of sleep and wakes up happily, there is every chance that he has had enough sleep. Even though it might be an early start, it is good that he feels content to come round gradually and wake up in his own time without needing you.

In this situation, you should leave him until he actually cries, and then if he seems fresh and wide awake, you should go to him, open his curtains/turn the light on and get him up for the day.

Sleep training at that time, after a long block of sleep and a chilled-out waking, is not likely to work and it may end up with him developing an unhappy association with his cot. The most effective solution would be if his naps were arranged so that it was possible for him to have a later bedtime without becoming overtired. He might then wake later in the morning.

To give an example: a 14-month-old baby, who naturally sleeps for ten and a half hours a night, has two naps and wakes at 2.30 p.m. from his afternoon nap, then settles happily to sleep for the night at 6.30 p.m. and wakes in a good mood at 5 a.m.

If he were to have both his morning and afternoon naps pushed later, so that his afternoon nap finished at 4–4.30 p.m., this would enable him to go to bed at 7.30 p.m. and wake at a more sociable 6 a.m.

Climbing out of the cot

For some very active children, as they approach their second birthday, there is a danger that they might climb out of their cot first thing in the morning and hurt themselves. Sometimes, lowering the mattress to the cot's bottom setting can be enough to prevent this happening. There are some very resourceful babies, however, who will simply use toys or a cot bumper to lever themselves up to the top of the cot bar and hurl themselves out.

If your baby is like this, you will need to move him into a small bed, and to consider placing a stair gate in his bedroom doorway, to keep him safe. Even then, at this young age, you will need to place the bed against a wall and place a soft removable cot side under the mattress and against the open side of the bed to prevent him rolling out as he moves around in his sleep.

Insight

Your baby does not sleep badly on purpose. If he is not sleeping well, you need to teach him the skills of how to sleep. The best way to do this is by getting to the root cause of his waking and then to gently and systematically change it.

Ten things to remember

1. Toddlers still need to sleep during the day, but between their first and second birthday, this may reduce to just one nap.
2. Be flexible when it comes to your baby's changing need to nap.
3. Dummies are not all bad news, but they outgrow their usefulness after 6–12 months.
4. If you can't face removing your baby's dummy, keep it for sleep only and teach him to self-manage it.
5. Early waking is common in toddlerhood and the most difficult sleep problem to overcome.
6. Well-rested toddlers are better able to play and learn.
7. Overtired toddlers may be even more unreasonable than normal!
8. Toddlers love rituals. This can work to your advantage (bedtime routine) or disadvantage (transfer to your bed).
9. Routines help toddlers to feel safe and secure.
10. One of the best parenting skills you can learn is to say no without humiliating your child.

6

Family life

Bringing up a family is both a privilege and one of the greatest challenges that any of us will ever face. Is it any wonder, given a task so important, so daunting and so *exhausting* that at times we question our ability to rise to the task?

When our children are small, we worry about their eating, their development and, perhaps most of all, their sleeping. As parents, we need our babies to sleep well, not only for their own sakes but for our sakes too.

Well-rested children are more likely to be content, secure and better able to play and learn. Well-rested parents are more likely to enjoy their children and have the energy to maintain other important relationships and interests.

Brothers and sisters

Having more than one young child to put to bed at night can present logistical difficulties: one child needs help with homework, another needs a story, a chat and a cuddle, and yet another needs a nappy change and a milk feed. Of course, it helps if the children have their own rooms and your partner is home in time to help with bedtime, but for many of us this is not possible. At the end of a tiring day, when everyone's levels of energy and humour are low, bedtime can become a time to dread rather than to enjoy.

> I love my children more than words can say, but at one point, when they were small, I used to live in fear of bedtime. The fact was that I needed the two of them to go to sleep by 7.30 p.m. so that I could have some time to myself. Bedtime

was always stressful and unhappy, and looking back, I think that they sensed my desperation and they felt rushed and pressured into sleep. I wish that I had taken the time to make bedtime a happier time for them and for me, too.

Of course, finding the energy to create a good bedtime routine to meet more than one child's needs is always going to be a challenge. If you are able to just give that tiny bit extra at the end of the day, however, it will repay you generously.

The first thing that you need to do is take some time to think about what you want bedtime to be like and then take some practical steps towards achieving this.

First, you need to establish a bedtime routine that is both consistent and meets your children's individual needs.

From the age of six months, if not before, your baby can be bathed together with her older sibling(s). It is perfectly all right to run a bath for your toddler, and while supervising him in the bath, you can 'dip' your little one into the water for her bath, too. You can then put her into her new nappy and nightclothes, on a clean towel on the floor, while you chat to and watch your older child in the bath. There is no need to have a separate baby bath or bath time for your little one.

After this, you can go to your children's bedroom, your own bedroom or, if your older child has a room of his own, to his room. While feeding your baby, you can read to your older one. We have seen already how it is wise to avoid allowing babies to fall asleep over their bedtime feed, so when your baby is fed but still awake, you should encourage a 'kiss goodnight' ritual and then take your baby to her cot. If this is in her own room, you should ask your older child to wait in bed for you to come back for your final kiss goodnight and cuddle.

Following the advice given in the previous chapters, you should settle your baby to sleep in a way that is appropriate for her age and then return to your older one(s) for a very brief but affectionate parting ritual.

It is important, whenever possible, for your older child to have some exclusive, loving time with you, however brief that might be. It can be hard for an older child to accept that you are giving the attention that was previously all his to a new baby. Try to make the time just before sleep a period of reassurance and special intimacy. You will feel so good about this, and so will he. If you somehow miss this time of comfort, your older child may not only fall asleep feeling unhappy, but he will look for this attention from you in other ways. It is very important when you leave your children for the night that you part on good terms.

There is no right or wrong answer when it comes to the question of whether it is best for brothers and sisters to share a bedroom. One advantage of sharing is that children often settle better and feel more secure at night in the close company of a sibling. Another lovely thing about siblings sharing a room is that they have a chance to develop their relationship in a natural way, often in the absence of their parents. They learn about sharing space, respecting privacy and belongings and about sharing secrets, too. Often, because of limited space, there is no other option than for children to share with one another. If this is the case, they might just be the lucky ones. Sharing a bedroom is a great preparation for nursery and school and, of course, for later life.

There are, of course, some drawbacks, too, the most obvious one being that, if one child is a poor sleeper, there is a risk that she might wake the other one up during the night or early morning. This is especially common in babyhood and, in particular, with twins, or with older babies and children when they are unwell. Later on, with toddlers and young children there is the issue of running amok after bath time and being too giddy and playful to settle down. Older children who share a room will inevitably experience conflicts over space and personal possessions from time to time.

Case study

Brother and sister who are both poor sleepers: improving their sleep skills and sharing a bedroom

Nicholas (26 months) and Jenny (12 months) were healthy and had no developmental difficulties, but their sleep and bedtime management were proving to be problematic.

The problem

- Nicholas needed to have his mother beside him every night as he fell asleep. As a consequence of this, he would wake later and need her to come and sit or lie beside him again in order to settle back to sleep. Inevitably, he would end up, at some stage during the night, in his parents' bed.
- Jenny was only able to settle if she was breastfed to the point of sleep each night. She subsequently woke up several times in the night and needed more feeds to help her resettle. Like her brother, she always ended up at some point in bed with her parents during the night.
- Their mother usually managed the bedtime routine alone and was finding meeting both children's needs very difficult. She wanted them both to share a room, but was worried that one child might wake the other and that their nights would be even worse.

The solution

- Both children needed to fall asleep at the beginning of the night without their mother beside them.
- They needed to find a bedtime routine that was less stressful and much more enjoyable.
- Both children needed to feel safe and secure in their own beds and not need to transfer to their parents' bed during the night.
- They would both benefit from sharing a bedroom together.

The plan

- Move both children into the same room. Place the cot parallel to Nicholas's toddler bed, position a chair in the middle, so that you can comfort both children if they cry. This will be a little disruptive in the short term, but eventually they will each benefit from the company. It will be logistically far easier for you to manage, too.
- Explain in simple and cheerful terms to Nicholas that he is going to have baby Jenny to sleep in his bedroom. During the day, move her cot into his room, and encourage the children to do a little

role-play game where they play at going to sleep or putting their toys to sleep. This should be kept very light-hearted.

- Bath them both together every night. Nicholas needs to get in the tub first, while Jenny is being undressed on the bathroom floor. Hold her and bath her in the shared water and sing a familiar bath-time song.
- After this, while still in the bathroom, put Jenny's pyjamas on. Give her a toy to play with while you get Nicholas out of the bath.
- Go directly to the children's room. Put on Nicholas's nappy and pyjamas while Jenny plays on the floor. After this, he can choose a book as the bedtime story.
- During the story, the three of you should sit on Nicholas's bed, and Jenny can have a breast feed. It is important that she doesn't feed to the point of sleep. Following this feed, encourage the children to kiss each other goodnight and then put Jenny into her cot. Nicholas should be tucked into bed directly afterwards. Turn the light right down and keep the room in soft semi-darkness. It is important at this stage that both babies are awake.
- This routine will be easier for you, as you will no longer need to run from room to room comforting each of them.

Nights 1 and 2

- Remain in the room comforting each child if they cry or are unable to go to sleep. Stay calm during this process. You are allowed to stroke and pat Jenny, for whom the change is greatest, and even lean right into her cot and put yourself close beside her. It is very important, though, that you keep her in her cot. Eventually Jenny will begin to give in to sleep. When she goes to sleep in her own cot, even if she has cried and even if you have been beside her, that is marvellous progress and she will be well on her way to sleeping through the night.
- As she enters sleep, you need to withdraw the amount of physical contact with her, so that you are just quietly sitting by her cot.
- During this process, you should keep Nicholas in his little bed next to the cot, and reassure him constantly, gently praising him and explaining what you are doing and that you are teaching Jenny how to sleep.
- If Nicholas is still awake once Jenny has settled, you need to remain beside him until he feels relaxed and tired enough to go to sleep.
- As Nicholas settles to sleep, you should just sit in a chair between the cot and his bed. Even if he cries and disturbs Jenny

after she has settled, you still need to help him go to sleep in his own bed.

- When Jenny first wakes up during the night, you should go to her and breastfeed her for a very few moments only. Do not allow her to fall asleep on the breast. After the shortened feed, place her back in her cot while she is still awake. Expect some crying, but try to demonstrate a calm and positive manner. Settle her in her cot as you did earlier in the evening, and do not bring her into your bed. Although this might be a hard habit to break, try not to be disheartened, as Jenny will very soon learn to be content in her own cot. If she wakes Nicholas, he should be reassured but kept in his bed.

- Repeat this each time Jenny wakes up. By not allowing her to fall asleep at the breast, you are breaking the suck/sleep dependence. By keeping her in her own cot, you are showing her that it is a safe and permanent space. She will very quickly overcome the expectation that she will be moving to your bed.

- If Nicholas wakes independently of Jenny, you should go to him as you usually do. If you need to stay with him, you can sit quietly as you did at the beginning of the night. It is most important, however, that he does not come into your bed; otherwise, he will lose the sense of safety in his own.

- In the morning, after first opening their bedroom curtains to show that it is now daytime, you should warmly welcome both Nicholas and Jenny into your bed. Give them both a sticker on their pyjamas as a reward for sharing a bedroom.

- After two or three nights of doing this, you will have already taught them new habits and you will be able to move on to the next stage.

Nights 3–7

- Keep up the new bedtime and settling routine, but move out of the chair between the children's cot and bed. At first, you need to potter around in the room and then gradually extend this pottering until you are moving very briefly out of, then back into, the bedroom.

- Once again, do not worry if one child disturbs the other – this will only happen while they are learning new sleep habits. Be warned that you may have to pop back in to them several times before they go to sleep. Eventually, they will both settle to sleep without you in the room ... you are nearly there now!

- During the night, if Jenny wakes for a feed, you can go to her and settle her by patting, etc. You should not offer her a night feed from now on. She doesn't need it and the expectation of a feed has been hampering her ability to settle and sleep well.

- By Night 7, after going through the children's normal routine and kissing them goodnight, you need to leave them and try not to go back in. You will have to listen out for them on the landing in case they become upset. By now, though, they will be used to settling with less help from you, and will be getting used to their new sleep set-up. If they cry, it will be in mild protest and last for a relatively short period. If necessary, go in every five minutes and stay for only 30 seconds.

- By this point, Jenny should have dropped her night feeds and be moving towards sleeping through the night.

The outcome

Nicholas and Jenny very soon grew to love sleeping in the same room together. It took about a week for them to get over the change in their bedtime routine and to settle to sleep in the same room. Their mother found the whole bedtime routine much easier to manage and she felt much more in control. Both children stopped waking in the night once she had managed to leave them to settle without her and had dropped Jenny's night feeds.

Soon, not only had bedtime improved, but before long the children were sleeping later in the morning, and when they woke up, they would play rather than cry to be brought into bed with Mummy and Daddy.

When they were brought into their parents' bed, they came as very welcome guests, and the parents started the day feeling well rested and delighted to see their two lovely children.

Conclusion

When there is more than one child in the family, it can be a help to have them in the same bedroom, provided they are taught good settling skills. From a parent's point of view, if the children are of a similar age, having them share a bedtime routine and a bedroom makes it easier to establish a happier settling process.

Bringing up your baby alone

Bringing up your child or children by yourself has its advantages, at least as far as sleep is concerned. You are able to focus more fully on your child's and your own needs and are free from the concern of caring for another adult. Having your baby in bed with you is less likely to be problematic, as is choosing to go to bed at the same time as your baby. There is no doubt that you alone have to cope when your baby wakes during the night, but the upside is that you do not have the additional stress or worry of her disturbing a partner.

When you have the responsibility of bringing up one or more children on your own, your friends and your family are very important. You should not be afraid to ask for help when you need it. Caring for a child day in and day out is completely demanding, however much you love her. If you are in paid work in addition to looking after your baby, you will know only too well how little time you have to yourself. Sometimes you will need someone to hold your baby for just half an hour while you have a bath or make a telephone call. While this might not be possible to organize on an ongoing basis, it is good to ask for support as regularly as you can.

The middle of the night presents its own special challenges, and if you are on your own with a crying baby, this time can occasionally feel very lonely and scary. Please follow the guidelines in this book to ensure that your baby is sleeping the best that she can for the age that she is. However, whether she is a good sleeper or not, it is important that you have a night off from time to time. One bad night's sleep will do no harm to your best friend, brother, sister or mother, and yet one good night's sleep will do you so much good.

Babies who sleep badly at home with their parents often sleep like a dream when staying at Grandma's or Grandpa's house. If this is the case with your baby, try not to feel undermined. It does not mean that you are a hopeless parent; it is merely that your baby has a different set of sleep associations in a different environment, and this can mean that she sleeps well during her 'sleepover'.

Twins and triplets

So far, we have considered the sleep needs of babies of various ages and habits. All of them present their own challenges, but nothing compares to the challenge of parenting twins, triplets or more. If you are to really enjoy your babies' miraculous infancy, it is important that both you and they get as much sleep as possible.

It is perhaps useful to follow the story of the first year of one couple, Julia and James, as they learned how to be parents to twins Amelia and (baby) James.

Julia describes the first few days after coming home from hospital with her babies as 'a nightmare!' She found it difficult to establish any kind of a routine, and felt that she was constantly having to ignore one baby while she dealt with the needs of the other one. Fortunately, she was well supported by her husband James, and together they muddled through this exhausting but amazing time.

After about eight weeks, they had introduced a bedtime routine, and both babies were sleeping for most of the night. Julia and James felt much more relaxed, in control and the babies were well rested and contented.

The secrets of their success were:

- The early introduction of a highly repetitive bedtime routine: Julia made good use of simple sleep cues such as songs, repeated phrases and a familiar sleep environment.
- After a milk feed at around 7 p.m., both babies would be put down awake. When they first did this, the babies would take some time lying awake, cooing, kicking and sometimes 'grizzling'. In a very short time this wakeful period got gradually shorter and both babies began to fall asleep quickly and easily.
- Before the babies were taking solids, Julia and James would wake them at around 10 p.m. for a second milk feed and

once again put them back in their cot, making sure that they were well winded and sleepy but awake.

- Baby James was a better sleeper than his sister Amelia. However, despite being in the same cot, he was rarely disturbed by his more wakeful sibling. This was because he was very accustomed to her presence and her sounds. Julia heartily recommends having baby twins sleep close to one another. She feels that it prevents them from feeling lonely in the middle of the night, and that the comfort that they gain from being near to each other means that they are less likely to need their parents.
- At first, Julia and James put the babies in a Moses basket each, placed 'top to tail' in the same large cot. They slept like this until they were 15 weeks old and then they were each given a separate cot, placed parallel to and very close to each other.
- After the 10 p.m. feed, nappies were changed in the night only if they were soiled.

One of the major difficulties with managing twins' sleep is how to cope with early waking.

As Julia and James found, at the beginning of the night, one wider-awake twin is unlikely to disturb the other one. This is because sleep is deeper in the early part of the night, and the sleeping twin is tired enough to ignore the familiar disruption going on around him.

However, at 5 a.m., sleep is lighter and one wakeful twin really can disturb the other sleepy one.

Many parents find the best solution is to bring the awake baby into their bed. Sadly, this often has negative repercussions, with the wakeful baby often rising earlier and earlier in anticipation of the move into the big bed. Some babies will even fail to settle at all in their own cots, feeling that they are merely in a temporary space that is not their 'real' bed.

For Julia and James, this was the beginning of a difficult period that took several months to resolve itself.

The best solution to this tricky situation is to keep both twins in their own cot(s), despite the disruption, your own sleep deprivation and the despair of your neighbours. You may find that, initially, you need to stay close by until the babies either go back to sleep or it is time for the day to begin.

Babies under six months or not yet taking solid food three times a day will sometimes require a milk feed at dawn. After this feed, it is important to put them back into their cot awake and encourage them to stay there until getting-up time (ideally at least 11 hours after their initial bedtime).

If you repeatedly allow your baby/babies to get up at dawn, they will never have the opportunity to learn to settle back off to sleep. You may need to sit quietly with them without playing or talking, but soothing them through the inevitable crying, until they eventually go back to sleep.

During this difficult period, it is important to go to bed early yourself, and be mentally prepared to get up at dawn when they wake, and invest this time with your babies. It makes sense that, if you have a supportive partner, you are able to share the burden of getting up early. Julia and James would alternate their 'dawn duty' and this prevented them from becoming exhausted.

Just after Amelia and James reached the age of one, they were sleeping through the night from 7 p.m. to 7 a.m.

According to their mother, 'One of the most wonderful things about twins is that they have each other. Unlike single babies, they do not suffer the loneliness of being left on their own to sleep through the night.'

Try not to worry too much about one twin or triplet being disturbed by the other(s). This is a transient period, and babies are amazingly resilient. If you are able to demonstrate a calm manner and to feel in control of the situation, your babies will feel calm and safe, too, and their distress will be minimal. They will soon benefit from a longer night's sleep.

> ## Guidelines for good sleep for baby twins and triplets
>
> - Let your babies sleep close to each other.
> - Follow a highly familiar bedtime routine.
> - Always put them in their cot(s) awake.
> - Do not allow fears of one disturbing the other lead you into a complicated night-time scenario of 'musical beds'.
> - Help them to feel safe by your loving, confident and consistent manner.

Adopted babies

If your first experience of parenting is with your adopted baby, you may feel daunted by the responsibility. It is very important for you to realize that all new parents feel the same way. One of your difficulties, however, is that you may have limited information about your baby's birth history or her family health history.

However, the really important information you need to help your baby sleep well is right in front of your eyes. When you are managing your baby's sleep, you need to respond to the signs and cues that she gives you. Your interpretation of these and your response to them is no less valid than if you were her birth parent.

When your new baby or toddler comes into your home, you need to gather as much information about her sleep as you can.

- Does she have a dummy?
- Does she have a night feed? If so, at what time?
- Does she have a comfort blanket or favourite toy?
- Does she sleep with the light on?
- Does she like to be rocked to sleep?
- Does she settle all by herself?

You may want to change some of her sleep rituals, and this is fine. You need to know what she is used to, however, before you go ahead.

Case study
Two-year-old boy, recently adopted: learning good sleep skills
Brett was adopted by Francesca and Sue when he was 18 months old. Before adoption, he had been in foster care from the age of three months. His new parents knew very little about his birth and early history; only that his birth mother was very young and had problems with drug abuse. He had had developmental delay until the age of a year, but now he was reaching the same milestones as his peers.

The problem
- Although his foster mother reported that Brett had always been a good sleeper with her, he had never slept through the night since coming to his new home.
- Frankie and Sue had blamed this on his anxiety at the change and had taken care to offer him lots of reassurance, especially around bedtime. It had become a pattern that, at bedtime, after his stories and milk, he would be held in one of their arms until he went to sleep and then placed in his cot. He would wake later, crying and looking for her.
- It took up to an hour to resettle him and this happened sometimes more than once in the night.
- Quite understandably, Frankie and Sue put Brett's night-time behaviour down to anxiety caused by his early life experience, which he was unable to express in any other way.
- This may have been the case to some extent, but the waking and crying was also typical of any two-year-old child who is rocked to sleep only to wake up later and find himself alone.

The solution
It was decided that Frankie and Sue would teach Brett how to settle to sleep at night without either of them beside him. This was a very worrying prospect for them, as they felt that he needed lots of reassurance in order to sleep. It was explained that it was, in fact, more traumatic for him to wake up and find himself alone than it would be for him to fall asleep without either of them there in the first place, providing they withdraw their presence in a sensitive and gradual way. The family was receiving counselling and support, arranged through the adoption agency, and Brett was expressing his feelings very well through his (rather beautiful) drawings. The signs were that he was a happy and well-balanced little boy.

The plan

- During the day, Frankie and Sue were asked to role-play with Brett by putting his toys into his bed, tucking them up and then leaving. They were all to praise the toys for going to sleep all by themselves.
- Also during the day, they were to tell Brett that he would be going to go to sleep in his own bed all by himself like a big boy. They needed to be positive when they told him this and to meet any protest with good humour.
- After his usual bath-time ritual, either Frankie or Sue was to read a maximum of three stories to Brett, with him cuddled up on their knee. They needed to keep the final storybook the same each night. This familiar ritual would help to create a feeling of security.
- When it was time to leave him, they were to use a little verbal ritual like 'Rock you for a minute now'. Either of them could then rock him for a moment or two and then gently place him in his cot – while he was still awake.
- After that, they were asked to stay beside him as he fell asleep in his cot. They were warned that he would stand up and cry, as he sought the familiar ritual of being held in one of his parent's arms as he fell asleep. This was bound to pull on their heartstrings, but they needed to be aware that his need to be rocked to sleep was habitual rather than emotional. After an hour or so, Brett would fall asleep in his cot, and they were asked to remain close beside him as he did this.
- For three nights they were to settle him in this way before beginning to move away. Once he was accustomed to falling asleep in his cot, this would not be as difficult as they imagined it might be.
- For the next four nights they were asked to move a little farther away from the cot each night, so that by night 7 they were sitting by the door as he fell asleep.
- On the following week they were asked to position a chair just outside his door after following their new bedtime routine and saying goodnight to him. Each time he called for them, they could either briefly return to him or simply call back, 'I'm just here, Brett.'
- It was very important that, when they returned to him, they did not allow themselves to be drawn into negotiations about position of toys, another story/cuddle, etc. It is really difficult to refuse a cuddle, so they were asked to give the briefest hug and then say, 'Big cuddles in the morning!'
- After being reassured many times, Brett would eventually go to sleep. When he did this, it was essential that they were not in the room with him.

- If Brett woke up during the night, they were to go to him immediately and reassure him. They were to be positive in their response to him and tell him he was a clever boy for staying in his own cot. They should then leave him to settle back to sleep without either of them in the room, returning to reassure him every five minutes if needed.
- In the morning, they were to first open his curtains before getting him out of his cot, then heap praise on him for going to sleep by himself. They were advised to give him a sticker on his pyjamas or a little treat or toy with breakfast and to have these rewards already prepared, as it was vital that he received this positive reinforcement as soon as possible.

The outcome

Frankie and Sue were very reluctant to begin what they regarded as a harsh solution to Brett's sleep difficulties. Once they decided to implement the plan, however, they were determined to see it through. After one night of quite severe protest, Brett began to learn the skills of settling to sleep by himself. Within ten days, he was settling alone and had stopped waking during the night. He was better tempered during the day and seemed less 'clingy', too.

Conclusion

Even if your baby's sleep difficulty has arisen from an emotional, medical or situational issue, using a sensitive sleep technique which addresses the baby's behaviour will still work to solve the problem.

Provided that you have other measures in place to address any potentially emotional or psychological issues, it is safe and sensible to use a 'behavioural' approach to help solve your child's sleep problem. This is the case whether it is your adopted child or your birth child.

When it comes to caring for the sleep needs of your adopted baby, you – just like any new parent – will need to gather information from books, family, friends and professionals about how to care for her. Armed with this information, you can then start the fabulous process of 'learning on the job'.

Don't be frightened of the fact that she is not your birth child. You are her parent now. You wanted her very much and are getting to know her more each day. Because you are a loving adult and you have her very best interests at heart, you can safely follow your instincts when planning her care. Parenting is a learning process – for both adoptive and birth parents.

A guide for grandparents... and sisters, brothers, aunts, uncles and best friends

You owe it both to your child and to yourself to allow a trusted grandparent to care for her from time to time. It is lovely for your parents to have a baby to care for, and provided they are fit and coming to it fresh, the chances are that they will have the energy to cope with her needs, even if she is not a good sleeper. Allowing your baby to develop close relationships with them will be a real benefit and a life-enriching experience for them. Not only this, but allowing a trusted grandparent to look after your baby will give you a well-earned break when you need it. Don't forget that enabling your child to feel comfortable with other adults in the family will provide you with a reassuring back-up in case you are ever ill or need to be away from her for other reasons.

When you hand over the care of your baby for babysitting in your home or for an overnight stay in theirs, it takes planning and the confidence to step aside. You are leaving them in charge of the most precious thing in the world to you, so you need to trust them completely. It will make their task easier and help your baby to feel more secure if you are able to provide enough essential information, so that the needs on both sides can be met. You also need to accept that grandparent, with all their years of experience, may have their own ways of settling your child. Provided that their values and methods are broadly in line with your own, this really should not cause any problems. Babies from a very young age are able to differentiate and to understand, for example, that, while Grandpa might rock her to sleep, Daddy reads a story and puts her in her cot while she is still awake.

Top tips: sleepover success

- Make certain that your parents, or other carers, are clear about your baby's normal bedtime and the routine leading up to it.
- Send along some familiar items which your baby associates with sleep. These might include her usual bedding, a familiar toy or bedtime storybook.
- If your baby still has night feeds, be sure that you provide plenty of milk or formula. It is better to give more than she normally needs, just in case you are held up or she needs extra feeds to settle.
- Have her formula/milk safely and conveniently stored to cut down on bottle preparation time. Ready-made formula feed in cartons or frozen expressed breast milk is easier to prepare than powdered milk.
- In preparation for the visit, if possible, allow your baby to spend time alone with her grandparents during the day.
- The first time you leave your baby at night, stay fairly local, so that you can be home quickly if needed. Your parents will need to feel completely confident that they can care for your baby before you go away for the weekend, for example.
- Give them a number of ways in which they can contact you while you are out. This isn't a sign of mistrust, but a sensible precaution that increases everyone's confidence.
- Show the person who is looking after your baby that you have confidence in them. Tell them how much your baby loves them and how you trust them.
- Come back at the time that you said you would – not earlier and not later. This will help to build trust on both sides, too.

How does paid childcare fit into the picture?

Most of us at some point in our baby's life will rely on some form of paid childcare. As more and more families have both parents working, and as we increasingly live away from our parents and other close relatives, nannies, au pairs, nurseries, childminders and babysitters have become a normal part of our support network.

Frustratingly, babies who will not sleep well for their parents will often sleep well at nursery or with their childminder or nanny. Carers *and* parents need to be absolutely clear that this is not because the parents are doing things wrong, but simply because the baby has a different set of expectations, routines and rituals with her carer than she does with her parents, and this often results in different sleep behaviour.

The reasons why babies tend to sleep better in a formal childcare setting include:

- other babies and children 'modelling' good sleep behaviour
- a more formal and structured day, which allows babies to anticipate when sleep time is coming, and to become sleepy as a result
- less rocking or handling by a caregiver around sleep time.

For similar reasons, babies often settle to sleep more easily when put to bed at night by a nanny than with you. With a nanny, there may be less expectation of extended cuddles and parting rituals and thus a tendency on the baby's part to fall asleep more quickly and easily.

When you come home after work, the time with your baby in the evening is very precious to both of you, and you may want to cuddle or feed her to sleep at night. In addition, you may be less likely to be able to tolerate her 'grizzling' or crying before she goes off to sleep. If this is the case, you need to accept that your methods of settling your baby are different from those of your nanny, and that her sleep may differ as a result.

It is not harmful or confusing for your child to experience different settling practices with different people, but be aware that, after the first few weeks or months of her life, she will expect a consistent approach from the person who is settling her to sleep and will respond accordingly. So, while she may settle happily to sleep with just a brief cuddle from her nanny, she may protest if you settle her in the same way, if that is not what she is used to from you.

For this reason, it is usually unhelpful to ask a nanny or night nurse to teach your baby to sleep at night for you and not to be involved in the process yourself. What is likely to happen is that your baby will respond to the sleep training initiated by the helper but as soon as she leaves and you take over, your baby will be as unsettled as ever. She might have learned to sleep well, but not necessarily for *you*.

For sleep training to be successful, it needs to be carried out by the person who most often puts the baby to bed and tends her during the night.

> I was still breastfeeding Helena during the night at 18 months, and I was newly pregnant with our second child. Both my husband and I were working, and I was becoming exhausted, especially with all the night feeds. We decided to get help from a night nursing agency, who sent a lovely nanny to us who would sleep-train Helena. It took her just over a week to get Helena to settle to sleep at night without the breast and to drop all her night feeds.
>
> We were delighted, but as soon as I tried to settle Helena in the same way as the night nanny had done, she started to search furiously for my breast, and ended up settling to sleep as she had previously done and then waking up during the night for more!
>
> I realized that, if any one was going to help Helena to sleep well at night, it had to be me. It was very hard, but I followed the instructions that the night nanny had given me, and with lots of resolve (and tears) I managed to get there in the end. She now has a feed, a story, a cuddle from either myself or my husband and then goes into her cot awake and sleeps through the night.
>
> Having a night nanny was brilliant in that we had a whole week of unbroken sleep, but in the end I still had to sleep-train her.

For the relationship between carer and parent to work well to promote good sleep for your baby, you need to communicate with each other. One of the best ways of doing this is by asking the carer to keep a simple daily diary. The information in this should include details about:

- naps – times, duration and where the naps were taken
- meals and snacks – times, what food was given and the amounts taken
- nappy changes and when your baby has a bowel movement
- outings and activities.

You need to be very clear about what is happening around daytime naps. Often, because a baby sleeps so well for her child-minder or nanny during the day, she may not be tired enough to settle happily to sleep at night. If you know how long or late she has slept during the day, you can schedule her bedtime accordingly.

This is just one of the instances of how your baby will benefit from honest and open communication between you and her carer.

Ten things to remember

1. Having more than one child to put to bed means that a routine is more important than ever.
2. Look for ways of shortening and simplifying the routine so it becomes enjoyable for everyone.
3. With more than one child to settle, you need to develop very loving but brief goodnight rituals – don't expect too much of yourself.
4. It is good for brothers and sisters to share a bedroom. It helps with sharing and communication skills.
5. Twins need to be kept together wherever possible.
6. What might look like emotional pleas from your child for your attention during the night are often just habit based.
7. Parents are the best people to teach babies good sleep skills.
8. Adoptive parents are just as capable of this as birth parents are.
9. Open and honest communication between carers and parents is absolutely essential.
10. Parents of young children should not feel guilty about going to bed early!

7

Special babies

There are times when babies are particularly fragile and require extra care, especially at night. For many, this time of fragility and additional need is very temporary, lasting through a period of minor illness or a bout of teething, for instance. For others, it may last for a few weeks or months, as is the case with babies who have reflux or certain forms of infantile eczema. Some babies will need special care at night for much of their early childhood, as is the case for babies with Down's and some other syndromes, sensory impairment or longer-term medical conditions.

For all these babies, a good night's sleep is particularly important. They need to be well rested in order to cope with the challenges with which their conditions present them. Good sleep is important for you, too – for the very same reasons.

Sleep training such a 'special' baby needs to be approached in a very thoughtful and sensitive way. It is completely unacceptable as well as counterproductive to leave a child who is in discomfort to cry alone in his cot. Sleeping difficulties need to be addressed in gentle, gradual steps and combined with any recommended medical treatments.

When your baby is unwell or in pain, treating his discomfort must take priority above teaching him how to sleep through the night.

Teething

Although a natural process and not an illness, teething can cause pain and general discomfort. Babies typically cut their first tooth at around six months, but for some this might not happen until much later. Some babies cut their teeth earlier than this, and some are even born with some teeth.

Teething troubles: what are the symptoms?

- Red, sore-looking gums
- Baby wanting to chew on everything
- Excess drooling
- Red cheeks
- Loose bowel movements
- Baby pulling at his ears

Not all babies suffer during teething, but many do, and the discomfort they feel is invariably much worse during the night.

Important: some of the symptoms of teething can be indicators of more serious illnesses. If your baby has a fever (above 102°F or 39°C) or seems very unwell, you should always seek medical advice.

General irritability

Very often teething is responsible for the development or worsening of sleep problems in babies. If your baby is teething, there are measures which you can take which will ensure that, as soon as the acute phase of teething is over, you and your baby can enjoy a good night's sleep.

- During the day, make sure that he has lots of opportunity to bite and chew.
- Encourage him with finger foods, provided that he is old enough, choosing crusty bread, bagel and toast which has been allowed to cool and go soft but tough.
- Because cold has a numbing effect, let him chew on a teething ring and/or whole peeled or scrubbed carrots that have been kept in the fridge. However, never put his teething aids in the freezer.

When babies are teething, they tend to drool and this often leads to the skin around the chin and neck becoming very chapped and sore. To help with this:

- Change bibs frequently or use soft, dry muslin cloths or even bright cotton neckerchiefs that coordinate with his clothes.
- After meals and drinks, use warm water and soft dry cotton cloths to clean him rather than wipes that may sting.
- Don't forget to clean and dry the soft skin folds under his chin, where food and moisture can easily become trapped.
- A gentle barrier cream here will protect him even further.

Another feature of teething can be frequent loose bowel movements. This can often lead to the skin on his bottom becoming sore. To prevent problems in this area:

- Check and change his nappy frequently.
- Be aware that, if his bottom is sore, it will sting when he does a wee.
- Allow your baby to kick around without a nappy, sitting or lying down on a towel.
- Once again, when you clean him, avoid using harsh wipes. It is better to stick to warm water and cotton wool.
- Use a barrier cream and watch out for signs that his skin is becoming red and shiny.
- If you have been treating your baby's nappy rash for 48 hours and there is no sign of improvement, you will need to visit your doctor to check for signs of Candida infection (thrush). If they are found, they will require an antifungal cream. Thrush infections in the nappy area are just as common in boys as in girls. They have tendency to crop up in warm, damp areas – like nappies and under the chins of teething babies.

If you notice that your baby is pulling at his ears, this is often a sign of discomfort and can indicate inflammation within the ear. This is common during teething, but to be safe you will need to visit your GP who will establish the cause of the pain and then recommend a suitable painkiller. If the pain is caused by bacterial infection and not just teething, your baby may be prescribed an antibiotic.

> Jonathan was a happy, smiling baby who had always had a good bedtime routine and slept well during the night. During the day, he was full of smiles and only ever cried if he was tired or hungry. When he began teething at six months, it was as if he had had a personality change! He seemed to cry constantly, and I found it very difficult to comfort him. His mouth was clearly very uncomfortable and his gums were swollen. The constant drooling made his skin chapped and sore. He also suffered from diarrhoea and soon developed a nappy rash, which made matters even worse.

> During the day, he found relief by biting on his teething ring (and anything else he could put in his mouth). Night-time was a different matter, however. He would frequently wake up crying and was very difficult to comfort. He was usually very snuffly and had problems breathing through his little nose. We went to our GP, who was very helpful and seemed to understand that teething can be more than just a minor ailment. She gave us paracetamol medicine for bedtime and rash cream for his sore bottom. She also advised us to tilt up the head of the bed to help his night-time breathing.

> Fortunately the first bout of teething was the worst and passed fairly quickly. We are more confident now about how to handle it when it happens again, including how to manage any discomfort during the night. When Jonathan is not actively teething, his sleep is good. I think that this is because we have never comforted him by bringing him into bed with us or by reintroducing a night-time bottle.

Colic

Colic is a form of very severe tummy ache, occurring mainly during the late afternoon and evening. Babies who have colic tend to be very difficult to console during an episode. Feeding does not help, and the only thing that tends to have any kind of positive effect is carrying your baby around in your arms. This is very hard on all of you, and having to constantly hold and rock your baby in the evening can lead to future settling and sleep problems.

Infantile colic is a common condition in very young babies, and although it can be really dreadful to manage, babies tend to grow out of it by the age of three or four months.

The crying which comes from colic can be alarming – especially when it first happens. *It is essential that colic is diagnosed only after other more serious conditions have been ruled out. If you are in any doubt at all, you should seek medical advice.*

Signs and symptoms of colic

- All the threes:
  - crying for more than three hours per day
  - crying for more than three days per week
  - crying for longer than a three-week period.
- Typically starts at around two to four weeks old.
- Baby cries often at the same time each day – usually in the evening.
- Sometimes you can hear or even see your child's stomach rumbling.
- Sometimes excessive 'wind' is produced.
- Baby tends to pull his knees up towards his tummy and strains while he cries.

Once you have a diagnosis of colic, you will need to go about managing it as best as you can. There is no recognized medical treatment for this condition, although there are steps that you can take both to minimize your baby's discomfort and to help you cope.

Top ten colic management tips

1 If you can anticipate when your baby is going to have a colicky episode, arrange if possible for a friend, family member or your partner to be around to help you.

2 Get a good-quality sling, and hold your baby in this as you walk around with him. It will be far less tiring on your arms, and he will benefit from being upright and close to you.

3 If there is a history of cows' milk intolerance in your family and you are breastfeeding, try eliminating cows' milk protein from your diet for a while.

4 If you are breastfeeding, watch out for signs of colic that are triggered by certain foods that you eat. You may need to cut out spicy and acidic foods, certain strong vegetables or dairy products.

5 If your baby is formula fed, discuss with your health visitor or GP changing to a different formula.

6 Always wind your baby well after his feeds. Slow, strong circular strokes to the base of his back are more effective than little taps on his upper back.

7 If you are using bottles, consider adopting an anti-colic system. This involves using a collapsible bag inside the bottle and limits the amount of air that your baby swallows.

8 Use the right-sized teat for your baby to make sure that the formula flow is neither too fast nor too slow – both of which may cause him to swallow excess air.

9 By all means, try homoeopathy or some of the over-the-counter colic remedies that are available from your pharmacy.

10 Sometimes a warm bath will help to comfort your baby when he has tummy pain.

Colic and sleep

Many colicky babies, after a period of intense crying in the evening, tend to settle and sleep well for the early part of the night. Partly this is because crying is extremely tiring and he is, quite simply, worn out.

It is not unusual, however, for a colicky baby to wake sometime later, either for his feed or before his feed is due, and need to be resettled for an extended period. This is not necessarily because he has tummy ache; it is more likely that it is because he has become used to falling asleep in your arms and knows no other way to settle himself.

Given that colic rarely lasts beyond four months, it is advisable that you give your baby the contact he needs during these early weeks, despite this not being conducive to good sleeping. He really does need to be held close to you during an evening colic episode, and if you rock him to sleep at the beginning of the night only to refuse to do so later, you will only cause him to feel confused.

There is no doubt that babies who have suffered from colic in the early weeks tend to develop sleep problems later, but there is little that you can do about that at the time. It is better to be aware that, when he has grown out of the colic, you will need to make some changes to his night-time settling routine. Don't worry – he will still be young enough to learn how to sleep beautifully.

> When Antonia was about two weeks old, she developed evening colic. It was a really tough time for all of us as she was so difficult to comfort. I felt exhausted and demoralized, as I was so helpless to ease her pain. We spent weeks just pacing up and down the living room with her, and it was impossible to ever put her down, even for a moment. It said in all the baby books that I should be putting her into her cot while she was still awake, but this was impossible for us. I worried that we were creating 'a rod for our own backs', but there was absolutely no other option.

> The colic began to improve when she was about three months old. We were relieved about this, but we also realized that she was still difficult to settle to sleep and she woke up constantly during the night for cuddles. Once we were confident that she was not in pain, and she was waking

merely out of habit, we set about teaching her to go to sleep more independently at bedtime.

This involved starting a very structured bedtime routine and then rocking her for a few moments until she was sleepy but not actually asleep. We would then put her into her cot and pat her until she went to sleep. She would protest at first but soon got the hang of it. For a time, she continued to wake during the night – even when she was not due for a feed – and we needed to pat her again. As, however, we began to withdraw our contact with her as she went to sleep at bedtime, she then began to sleep through the night. We now have a very content and well-rested baby, and those 'Colic Days' feel like ancient history.

Reflux

What we commonly call 'reflux' is known in medical terms as 'gastro-oesophageal reflux'. It is condition that, thankfully, is being increasingly recognized and treated. It is most common in the first six months to one year of life. The vast majority of babies naturally grow out of their reflux and suffer no future digestive problems.

What happens in reflux is that the contents of a baby's stomach leak back into the oesophagus (food pipe or gullet) and cause posseting (bringing up small amounts of milk), vomiting and/or a burning pain (heartburn) due to the acidity of the stomach's contents. This is because the valve (lower oesophageal sphincter) between the oesophagus and the stomach is often not yet fully working in babies. With maturity, it becomes more efficient, although this may take up to a year or a little longer.

Sometimes reflux (especially 'silent reflux', where there is no significant vomiting) can be confused with colic, as many of the symptoms are similar, including the age of onset – two to four weeks. Unlike colic however, reflux, although more serious, can be treated.

Signs and symptoms of reflux

- Poor feeding: your baby may refuse feeds, as feeding may cause discomfort
- Poor weight gain: as a result of poor feeding
- Vomiting and posseting (very demoralizing if you have struggled to get your baby to take a feed)
- Crying, drawing his knees up and arching his back after feeds
- Coughing
- Difficulty settling to sleep

If you suspect that your baby has reflux, you must seek medical advice and a proper diagnosis. Although the reflux cannot be cured, it can be controlled. Your baby's symptoms can be improved, which is very important so that he can enjoy his food and his sleep.

Your doctor may recommend agents to thicken his feeds or to control the acid production in his stomach. She may even suspect that the reflux is linked to a cows' milk allergy and suggest that you try a different feed. While you take the medical advice that is offered to you, you can employ some simple comfort strategies of your own.

Top tips: reflux management

- Hold your baby in an upright position during his feed and for at least half an hour after it.
- Try not to rush your baby's feeds. Allow him to take things at his own pace and be prepared to feed him little and often if that's what he wants.
- Allow him to have a dummy or to suck his thumb. Swallowing may help ease his discomfort.
- When putting him in his cot, place him with his feet right at the bottom. Then tilt the top of the cot, so that his tummy and chest are higher than his feet. This will help prevent his stomach contents from spilling upwards.
- Lying flat makes the pain of reflux worse, so, as with the cot, make sure that his pram is also tilted downwards.

- During the day, allow him to sit semi-upright in a baby chair.
- Invest in a good-quality, well-fitting baby carrier (sling) so that, when your baby is unsettled and has pain, you can keep him upright and close to you.
- Accept any offers of help from trusted family or friends. Caring for a baby with reflux can be a real challenge and you will need a break from time to time.
- When you start to introduce solid food, ask for specific advice from your health visitor or doctor. Avoid acidic foods for obvious reasons, and take heart that, once solid food is established, the symptoms of reflux often improve.
- Try not to get down-hearted. Your baby is more than likely to grow out of this condition very soon.

Reflux and sleep

As with colic, if your baby is in pain at bedtime, you may need to hold him until he is comfortable enough to go to sleep. As reflux tends to last longer than colic and, to some extent, can be helped by positioning, sensitive feeding and medication, there is a little more that you can do to prevent future sleep problems from developing.

As with all babies, you need to observe the principles of promoting good sleep, such as a consistent bedtime routine, a comfortable and quiet sleep environment and a cosy cot. In addition to this, you need to schedule your baby's bedtime feed so that he is able to digest it before you put him in his cot. You also need to take into account how long any medication may take to work. For this reason, it may be necessary to have a slightly earlier bedtime routine and to take longer over it, too.

> Sasha was diagnosed with reflux at about 16 weeks. Before that, we were told that she had colic and would grow out of it. She didn't grow out of it, however, and we were relieved finally when our doctor explained to us why she was so unsettled. I think that, as she was not a typical 'sicky' baby, no one had thought that her problems might be caused by reflux. This resulted in a delay in her reflux being identified. I was frantic

that she had not gained enough weight and had found feeding her to be really upsetting, as she seemed to hate her milk. Once she was diagnosed and given the medicines, I noticed the difference in her almost immediately. She became much more settled and content. We were given advice on how to position her slightly upright in her cot to ease her discomfort and how we should hold her erect after feeding her.

Once her treatment was established, she began to sleep much better at night. I think that this was partly as a result of her feeding better during the day, and partly because we were able to put her in her cot to go to sleep rather than holding her in our arms.

I would urge all parents with babies who are not feeding well and crying a lot to seek medical help. I wish that we had identified the reasons for Sasha's feeding and settling problems earlier.

Once your baby's treatment for reflux is established, you need to make sure that he is placed in his cot at the beginning of the night while he is awake and then comforted there. After any night feeds, you need to hold him upright to allow the feed to go down and then place him back in his tilted cot (with a dummy if necessary) and allow him to self-settle if he possibly can.

Head banging and other rhythmic movements

About two thirds of healthy babies demonstrate 'sleep related rhythmic movements'. These can be body rolling, head rolling or even head banging – and are the ways that some babies like to settle themselves to sleep. These night time movements are almost always harmless. Many babies bang their head against the side of the cot as a prelude to sleep.

Alarming as it might appear, head banging is rarely a sign of emotional distress and is usually a simple self-settling device that babies use. Believe it or not, head banging is similar to rocking, and the rhythmic nature of the banging provides a similar comfort to being rocked in someone's arms or pushed back and forth in a pram. Most babies grow out of this behaviour between the ages of two and four years.

Head banging can often occur when a baby is teething or has an ear infection – perhaps to distract him from the discomfort that he feels.

Although head banging can be associated with sensory problems such as visual or auditory impairment, and with learning disabilities, it is not the major signal of these conditions and is also very common among physically and mentally healthy babies.

Sometimes, a baby who bangs his head and causes anxiety to his parents can learn that head banging leads to a predictable and rewarding outcome, such as being lifted from the cot, given a feed or being brought into his parent's bed.

While the initial point of the head banging might not have been to seek this kind of outcome, the head banging can soon become a means to an end – for the baby to obtain a certain reaction from his parents. It must be stressed that this is in no way a manipulative act on the part of the baby, but merely a learned response and a seeking of the familiar.

Case study

Twenty-two-month-old baby girl: banging her head at bedtime

Tatiana had recently become a big sister. Her baby brother Jonathan was just a few weeks old. Apart from some feeding issues when she was quite small, Tatiana had had a trouble-free babyhood. She was a bright, happy and well-developed toddler and had recently settled well into part-time nursery. Her parents were sensitive to her emotional needs and were aware of the changes going on in her life – as was her live-in nanny, who had been with her since she was a young baby.

The problem

Tatiana had recently begun to bang her head against her cot when she was about to go to sleep. This had caused considerable alarm to her family, partly because it was a new behaviour and partly because they were afraid that she would seriously hurt herself. They were reassured that it was extremely unusual for such a small child to cause herself any significant injury, and were advised to continue with her excellent bedtime routine and to ignore the behaviour. They accepted this advice, but one night Tatiana was seen on the video monitor to hit her head very hard indeed. When her mother rushed to her, she found that she had a very large swelling on her head and some serious bruising. Della's concern was so great that she needed to seek a medical assessment. Although the injury was visible and the incident was extremely worrying, thankfully, no long-term damage had been sustained.

The family needed the head banging to stop, and could no longer ignore it and hope that it would go away on its own. To this end, one of Tatiana's parents would stay with her as she fell asleep in her cot or would bring her to sleep in their bed. However, each time they turned away from her for a moment, Tatiana would bang her head very hard, and they would lift her from the cot.

The solution

Given that this head banging could not be ignored, Tatiana's parents decided to employ behavioural techniques to stop her head banging. This approach often involves ignoring the unwanted behaviour and rewarding the good. In this case, however, the undesirable behaviour could not be ignored. A system was introduced where, under close supervision, a mild disincentive was introduced each time Tatiana tried to bang her head.

The plan

- Tatiana's cot bars were covered with safe cot rail padding. This was a safeguard in case she banged her head before she could be stopped.
- After following her normal bedtime routine, Tatiana was to be placed in her cot as normal and the lights turned down so her room was dark (as it usually was).
- After saying goodnight, her parent was to leave the room but wait out of sight and in silence by the door.
- If Tatiana banged her head, the parent was to return to her quickly and silently and lift her from the cot. She was to sit on the carpeted floor rather than be held in her parent's arms.
- The parent would remain in the room with her but would offer no conversation or cuddles. At first, Tatiana tried to bang her head on the bedroom floor, but her father or mother would say firmly, 'No!' and gently restrain her from doing it again if she tried. Once she stopped attempting to bang her head, they were advised to place her back in the cot.
- Each time she banged her head, she was to be lifted out again and spend five minutes sitting quietly on the floor. As the room was very dark, it was not possible for her to play with her toys.

- Eventually, on one of the occasions when she was placed back in her cot, she would go to sleep without banging her head. This might take time, but they were advised to remain calm and to stick with it.
- As Tatiana learned that the outcome of banging her head was not as good as when she didn't bang it, she would soon learn that head banging was not a good idea.

The outcome

It was Tatiana's father who implemented the sleep plan initially, as her mother found the whole thing too emotionally charged and stressful. Once the plan was put into practice in a consistent and confident way, it took Tatiana only a night or two to realize that being in her cot was cosier than sitting on her bedroom floor. She very soon understood that being in her cot meant that she was not allowed to hurt herself. Once she had figured this out, her head banging in the cot soon stopped completely.

Conclusion

Although head banging is mostly harmless, it can on occasion cause real concern. Tatiana's parents were very worried about Tatiana's physical and mental well-being, especially with all the changes that had happened in her life recently (new baby, new nursery). By supervising and monitoring her head banging very closely and by neither ignoring nor rewarding it, the family were able to eliminate it altogether. They are aware that the head banging may possibly be associated with emotional issues and are working closely with her nursery to monitor her happiness and well-being. She still uses a rhythmic element as a sleep prompt, but this now involves singing and moving her legs up and down.

Vomiting

Babies and toddlers have a very sensitive vomit reflex, and vomiting very often happens during coughing or crying. Some babies have more of a tendency to vomit than others and if you are teaching your baby how to sleep independently, his tendency to vomit when left may well put you off leaving him to cry.

Vomiting in babies can be a sign of illness, such as a tummy bug, food intolerance/allergy, reflux, asthma, ear infection or fever. If your baby is otherwise well, however, vomiting only when left at bedtime is usually a learned behaviour.

> Nathalie was never really a 'sicky' baby, but the first time
> that we left her to cry herself to sleep at bedtime, she was so
> violently sick that we gave up at once, feeling terribly guilty
> and vowing that we would never do that to her again.

A common scenario when sleep training is that the baby vomits, is taken out of the cot, cleaned, soothed and fed again, and then allowed to fall asleep either during his second feed or in his parent's arms afterwards. While this is an utterly natural response on the part of parents, it needs to be said that, from the baby's point of view, vomiting that is rewarded in this way soon becomes a learned response to being left alone.

It is hard to do, but if your baby throws up during sleep training, a better response is to gently but quickly clean him, change the bedding and then place him back in his cot without offering another feed or cuddling him to sleep, and then carry on where you left off or if you've been doing a controlled crying method, switch to gradual withdrawal instead. It is safe to do this if your baby is otherwise healthy and is over six months old.

Case study
Thirteen-month-old baby girl: vomiting when left alone at bedtime

The problem
Georgina had been breastfed to sleep until the age of eight months. She moved on to formula after this, and at bedtime, after her feed, her mother would climb into the cot with her (not as uncommon as you might think!) and cuddle her until she went to sleep. Later in the night, Georgina would wake up and cry until her mother got back into the cot with her.

Neither parent was happy with this arrangement, but they were afraid to do anything else. The reason was that they had tried 'controlled crying' once, and Georgina had got so upset that she had vomited. Taking this as a sign of real emotional distress, they had vowed never to leave her to cry again.

The solution
Georgina's parents needed to understand that her vomiting had been a mechanical response, triggered by her crying. They needed to teach her how to go to sleep by herself. They had to be prepared for her to vomit and to respond in a confident and helpful way, so that vomiting didn't become a learned response to being left alone.

The plan

- Give Georgina a beaker of milk (approximately 6 fl. oz/180 ml) with her supper.
- After this, allow her to play for at least half an hour before her bath.
- Go directly to her room after her bath and then give her a small amount of milk (3 fl. oz / 90 ml) in a bottle.
- Just one of you should then read her a story/stories after her milk. The final story should be the same one each night.
- Meet any resistance to the new routine with confidence and humour.
- Throughout the bedtime routine, consciously use key phrases/songs, etc., as these will become part of her system of sleep cues.

Nights 1–3

- After the last story, develop a little 'kiss goodnight' phrase or ritual, then place her in her cot and be prepared to stay beside her until she settles to sleep. When she cries, you can give her as much physical contact as she needs. Eventually, her crying will subside and she will lie down. Praise her as she does this.
- If she vomits:
  - Just one of you should deal with her.
  - Be as calm as possible, as you quickly change her bedding. Do not bath her again, but bring a warm flannel and just wipe her hands, face and hair if necessary.
  - Offer her a small drink of water – but do not give her another bottle.
  - Throughout this process, you should keep the bedroom lights down low.
  - As soon as she is clean and you have changed her sheets, you should place her back in her cot and leave her to settle to sleep with one of you still beside her but not in the cot with her.
  - Remember that the vomiting is not a sign of illness, and you are probably a lot more distressed about it than she is. You need to try not to reward her behaviour with lots of attention.
- Once she has gone to sleep, go to bed yourself and be prepared to be up with her during the night.
- When she wakes, you should settle her in the same way as you did at the beginning of the night. Remain calm and resolute.

Nights 4 and 5

- By now, Georgina will have overcome her expectation that you will lie down beside her until she goes to sleep, and will have learned that any vomiting is not going to lead to another feed or to you getting into the cot with her. You can now begin to reduce the contact that she has from you as she goes to sleep.

- Lay her down in her cot and then potter around the room, tidying up, and so forth. It is OK to return to her if she needs you to, but you must reduce any physical contact.
- If she wakes during the night, you can go to her and, after you have settled her down, sit beside the cot as you have done earlier, but with reduced physical contact.

Night 6 onwards

- Keep up the new bedtime routine, then extend the 'pottering' so that you leave the room for a moment or two. At first, you should leave for a very few seconds and then return whether she is crying or not. Georgina needs to feel reassured that you are close by.
- Any vomiting should be treated in the same matter-of-fact manner as earlier.
- As the nights progress, you are to leave the room for longer periods. Georgina may grumble or complain, but by now, with all the groundwork that you have done, these complaints are less likely to lead to vomiting and will be nowhere near as distressing as the 'controlled crying' had been.
- Once she has learned to fall asleep at the beginning of the night without having you in her cot with her, she will find it much easier to sleep through the night.

The outcome

On the first day of the new gentle sleep training programme, Georgina vomited twice at the beginning of the night and once during the night. It was very difficult for her parents to stick with the sleep plan, but they supported one another, and feeling confident that she was not unwell or feeling abandoned and frightened, they were able to remain on task.

On the second night, Georgina did not vomit at all, even though she still cried a little. From then on, her parents felt increasingly confident about implementing the sleep plan. It took two weeks before they felt able to leave Georgina alone in her room to settle, but they managed to do it in the end. As soon as they were able to leave her to self-settle, Georgina slept the whole way through the night.

Conclusion

Babies who vomit when left to cry benefit from gentle and gradual withdrawal techniques. Parents should not be afraid of the vomiting, because if it is treated calmly and left unrewarded, it will usually resolve itself.

Top tips: vomiting at bedtime

- Do not panic, or this will alarm your baby.
- Just one of you clean up.
- Keep the lights low and your voice calm.
- Do not take him out of the room.
- Offer a small drink of water but no more milk.
- As soon as your baby and his cot are clean, place him back into his cot.
- Do not treat the vomiting as a sign of illness if he is otherwise well.

Very rarely there are babies whose vomiting behaviour is so severe that, if left, there is a danger that they will carry on until they are dehydrated. If your baby vomits more than four or five times when left alone, you need to:

- seek a medical opinion to rule out any underlying physical cause
- withdraw your presence in an even more gradual way than outlined in the case study above
- still respond in a calm manner to the vomiting.

Eczema

The most common kind of eczema in young babies is the *seborrhoeic type*. This is also known as 'cradle cap', although it can extend from the scalp to the eyebrows and face. It might look unpleasant, but this type of eczema is not usually itchy and most babies grow out of it in the first few months of life. It is rarely the cause of sleeping problems.

The other kind of eczema is the *atopic type*, which is itchy and uncomfortable. This eczema is linked to allergies: usually to substances in the environment coming in contact with baby's skin, but sometimes to food as well. Eczema is more common in babies than in adults, and this means that the majority of babies will outgrow their condition before they reach adulthood.

If your baby has atopic eczema, there is a chance that at some time his sleep is going to be affected by it. The most disruptive aspect of eczema on sleep is the constant itching and desire to scratch. As a parent of a baby with eczema, you will know that, if he has spent the night awake and scratching, his skin is likely to be much worse in the morning. For this reason, it is natural that, when you know he is awake, you will do anything to help him stop scratching and soothe him back to sleep.

Although baby eczema can only be controlled rather than cured, there are some measures that you can take to minimize the disruption to your baby's sleep due to this common condition.

Top tips: managing eczema and sleep

- Use pure cotton clothing and bedding.
- Use a non-biological washing powder and avoid fabric conditioner. Machine-wash your baby's clothing. At the end of the wash, run an extra rinse cycle.
- Unless you have been advised not to by your specialist, bath your baby every night in not-too-hot water that is well moisturized.
- After the bath, while his skin is still warm and receptive, use a thick emollient cream on his skin.
- Keep his room and his bedding cool. Use light cotton layers as bedding.
- Vacuum his room each day and steer clear of heavily upholstered furniture, drapes and so on.
- Let your baby sleep on a hypoallergenic mattress.
- Place cotton mittens on your baby's hands and keep his fingernails short to reduce the damage caused by scratching.

Babies with longer-term medical conditions

One of the most difficult aspects of helping a baby who has a longer-term medical condition to sleep through the night is deciding whether the sleeplessness is caused by the illness or is merely habitual. Of course, with a vulnerable child, who may be in pain or other discomfort, it is wiser and kinder to err on the side of caution and blame the illness. However, if you feel that your baby is suffering from a lack of sleep, and that his medical condition is more difficult for him to cope with as a result of this, it makes sense to do your best to maximize his sleeping potential. Not only this, but as a parent of a child with an illness or disability, you need to get as much rest as you can in order to care for him to the best of your ability. As we have already seen, sleep training need not be harsh, and it is invariably more successful if the reason for your baby's sleeplessness is taken fully into account and sensitively addressed.

Pain

Sadly, some babies suffer from chronic pain, caused by a variety of conditions and medical treatments. It is absolutely vital that pain is treated effectively and that you discuss all possible options with your doctor or specialist. Treatment for pain need not always be with drugs (although, if drugs are recommended, you ought to follow your doctor's advice). Often, such things as massage, positioning, warm baths and complementary therapies can be very useful in the treatment of painful conditions, and these should be explored.

Once you are confident that your child's pain is under control, you need to teach him to sleep independently. If his sleep skills are robust, he is more likely to be able to sleep through any minor pain that he experiences during the night.

As always, it is sensible to teach your child how to go to sleep alone at the beginning of the night. After a warm bath, a dose of any necessary medication and a milk or formula feed, he is likely to be in his optimum state of comfort, and this is the right time to teach him how to go to sleep alone in his cot. 'Controlled crying' techniques (see Chapter 9) are not usually appropriate for babies who are susceptible to pain. For one thing, as his parent, your resolve may not be strong enough if you feel that his crying is due to pain rather than habit. For this reason, it is more acceptable and sensible to use one of the gradual withdrawal techniques that are discussed in Chapter 9.

Difficulty in breathing

Some longer-term medical conditions from which babies can suffer will cause difficulty in breathing. This is likely to worsen during the night, when your child is lying down. Coughing also has an adverse impact on a baby's ability to sleep through the night. As with pain control, it is important that your baby receives the best possible treatment to control his symptoms, whether this be with drugs or by other means. Some of the medicines used to treat breathing difficulties can have a stimulating effect and therefore cause further sleep problems. You will need to discuss with your doctor the possible effects of your baby's medication and its administration.

If your baby has difficulty in breathing, or has a tendency to cough during the night, there are certain practical steps that you can take to keep him comfortable.

Top tips: helping your baby to breathe at night

- First and most important is that you avoid him coming into contact with tobacco smoke, both during the day and at night. Do not allow anyone to smoke in your home even if they are downstairs and he is upstairs.
- Tilt up the top of his cot, by placing thick books such as telephone directories under the feet of his cot. However, make sure that he is positioned 'feet to foot' (see Chapter 2) to prevent him slipping down and suffocating under his bedclothes.
- Invest in a humidifier for his room. If this is not possible, boil a kettle in there for several minutes before he goes to bed.
- If your baby is over three months old, you can use preparations of menthol or eucalyptus. Impregnate a handkerchief with one of these and place it near the cot, or use one of them in conjunction with a steamer device.
- Have a drink of cool boiled water close to hand, to ease any coughing during the night.

In common with babies who suffer from painful conditions, it is important to teach babies with breathing difficulties how to go to sleep independently at the beginning of the night. If you are able to do this, it will strengthen his ability to settle if he wakes up during the night. After attending to your baby after a coughing or wheezing episode during the night, you will both be very tired. It is important that your baby is able to resettle himself once he is comfortable again, and that he doesn't rely on being rocked back to sleep in your arms, for instance.

Limited mobility

For some babies, limited mobility can be a serious cause of sleeping difficulties. This is not usually the case with babies who are born with a mobility difficulty, as these infants are amazingly proficient at adapting as they grow. The babies who are most likely to have problems with restricted mobility are those who find their movements suddenly limited – after breaking a bone or following a period of correctional orthopaedic treatment, for example. During this kind of treatment, you are faced with not only restriction in your baby's movements, but also possible pain and sometimes itchiness caused by a plaster cast.

To some extent, you need to go with this problem and treat the symptoms with medication, massage and positioning. If you are able to soothe your baby prior to sleep and not to the point of sleep, you will avoid any sleep problems from continuing once your baby is mobile again. Be aware that comforting your baby with unnecessary night feeds will cause future difficulties.

Hospital admissions

The disruption of frequent hospital admissions can have a negative impact on your baby's ability to sleep. Often, his sleep will be disturbed by a constant level of light, which limits his body's ability to recognize daytime and night-time cues. In addition, he may be frequently woken for medical observation of his vital signs or for the administration of drugs or other treatments. The normal bedtime routine will be disrupted, and he will lose the benefit of the familiar environmental cues that tell him that it is time for sleep.

While you are in hospital with your baby, the most important thing is that you make both him and yourself as comfortable as possible. Take as many familiar items from home as possible into the hospital with you if you can, especially those things with a night-time association that you can use for bedtime, such as a familiar teddy, mobile or night-time book. If you are able to bath your baby, do this before bed and use as many familiar verbal sleep triggers from your home bedtime routine as you can. These include the familiar bath-time song that you sing to him, goodnight phrases and so on.

Take heart in the fact that babies, even from a very young age, are able to recognize that there are different settling 'rules' when away from home from the normal ones. Babies who usually sleep well and settle without problems at home will often settle back into their usual sleep routine and settling habits once they are back in their own familiar environment.

Babies with learning disabilities or special needs

If your baby has a physical or mental disability, you may find managing his sleep especially difficult. Partly this comes from fear of the unknown: is he waking at night because of neurological factors or is he just in the habit of waking? In the first two years of his life, it can be unclear what the exact impact of his disability has on his capacity for sleep. It is true that babies who have certain syndromes or conditions such as visual impairment may have a tendency to sleep poorly. What is important, though, is that, if your child has sleep problems, you do not simply accept this as an inevitable part of his condition. The two may very well not be linked at all.

All babies benefit from a clearly laid-out system of sleep cues leading up to bedtime (a bedtime routine). For babies who have learning or physical difficulties, it is even more important that this routine is utterly consistent as well as multisensory.

If your baby is presented with a variety of physical sleep cues leading up to bedtime, he is more likely to understand and learn that sleep is coming soon.

For many babies with a learning disability, it can take longer for a bedtime routine to become meaningful. If you can make the bedtime routine as rich and as consistent as possible, you will definitely speed up the learning process for him.

Bedtime routine – a multisensory approach

Sight Use visual sleep prompts, such as dimming the lights and following a familiar pattern of actions (a song in the bath accompanied by actions, closing the curtains, etc.). These are very helpful sleep triggers for all children except those with profound blindness.

Hearing Use the same phrases and songs at each step of your bedtime routine. These verbal sleep prompts will help to reinforce the familiarity of a bedtime routine and are useful to all children except those with a serious hearing impairment.

Touch A warm bath, a gentle massage, changing into a soft sleeping suit and a loving cuddle – these are all examples of how the sense of touch will tell your baby that sleep is coming soon.

Smell Use familiar bathing products, massage lotions and skin creams in preparation for bedtime. Try to keep these for night-time only and use other products for daytime cleansing and nappy changes. Lavender has been recognized for many years as having a calming effect.

Taste The familiar taste of toothpaste, for instance, and night-time medication and warmed milk will all act as sleep triggers if they are experienced in the same order each night.

Night-time sleep training should be gentle with any baby, but especially so with those babies with special needs. You should aim to be as consistent and predictable as possible both in settling your baby and in responding to his night-time waking. This will help him to feel safe. If you are planning to drop night feeds, or to teach your baby how to settle by himself in his cot, you should always plan to make the changes with gradual and gentle steps.

During meetings with his doctor, you should discuss your baby's sleeping habits if you are having problems. Sleep is highly important to any baby's growth and development, but is particularly significant for those with special needs. It may be that a medication he is taking is having an impact on his sleep, for example, and your doctor will be able to advise you about this.

You may even be advised to use a medicine specifically designed to help him sleep. Your doctor will also be able to tell you what is safe or unsafe for your child in terms of sleep training.

Sadly, there are some babies who at times will need 'round the clock' care to keep them safe and comfortable. If your baby needs this, you should seek out all the help you can get. This includes statutory services from health or social care organizations as well as help from trusted family, friends and voluntary groups. If you are able to get some rest yourself, you will be better able to enjoy your child and to meet his needs.

Except in the case of a very severe physical difficulty, chronic sleepless nights need not always go with the territory of having a child with a learning disability.

Ten things to remember

1. Attending to your child's discomfort should always take priority over sleep training.
2. Teething and other ailments tend to be worse during the night.
3. Colic is distressing but temporary.
4. Reflux tends to go on for longer than colic but the symptoms can be treated.
5. Any crying that is prolonged, persistent or different sounding should be medically assessed.
6. Babies who regularly vomit when crying are likely to be doing this as a learned response.
7. It is important not to automatically blame a baby's poor sleep on a pre-existing condition. There may be a completely different cause.
8. Multisensory bedtime routine is important for most babies, but especially for those with special needs.
9. If your child is receiving ongoing medical care, you should always discuss sleep as part of the treatment plan.
10. Caring for an unwell or disabled child is hard work. Please remember your own sleep needs. Accept and ask for offers of help.

8

Getting ready for change

One of the most difficult aspects of helping your baby to sleep better at night is contemplating the seemingly overwhelming changes that you need to make. It is difficult enough, coping with your baby's constantly changing needs during the day, in terms of feeding, playing and so on. By the time it gets to bedtime, most parents, quite understandably, are tempted to take the line of least resistance. If your nights with your baby are bad, then the prospect of them getting worse can be an unbearable thought.

Remember, though, that if your nights are already difficult, you have little to lose.

Keeping a sleep diary

Before commencing sleep training of any kind, it is advisable that you first keep a diary of your baby's sleep. Ideally, you should do this for a week before you begin the sleep training.

The diary need not be complicated but it should be completed honestly and be written up at the time. You may not feel like completing a diary in the middle of the night, but the fact is that writing up events the morning after may mean that your information is not accurate. If both you and your partner take it in turns to attend to your baby during the night, you both need to fill in the diary.

What a sleep diary will show you

Sleep diaries reveal:

- a realistic overview of your baby's sleep
- the times when she naturally wants to sleep

- whether there is a relationship between certain foods/activities and her sleep
- under what conditions she is likely to sleep best
- what (if any) her sleep triggers are.

Sometimes the mere action of keeping a diary will help you. The record may show you that your baby's sleep is, in fact, usual for her age and will reassure you that she is 'normal'.

Keeping the diary may highlight an obvious cause of her poor sleep – for example, over-napping during the day or incorrect wake windows leading to settling problems at bedtime. If this is the case, the solution is easy – you just need to adjust her daytime naps. No formal sleep training will be necessary.

It is not at all unusual for the very action of keeping a diary to have a direct and positive influence on the way you address your baby's sleep needs. By adopting a more organized approach, you may find that you solve your baby's sleep problem without even knowing that you are doing it.

Your diary should be tailored to meet your child's and family's needs. For example, if night-time sleep is not a problem, you only need to document daytime events. Feel free to design the layout and content of your personal sleep plan, but here is an example that you might like to use.

Sample sleep diary

Morning wake-up time Where did she wake?	Monday 6.30 a.m. in our bed.
Morning Food taken. What time? Time, length and place of nap(s). How did you settle her? How long did it take?	7 a.m. porridge – not interested – 2 tsp. 8.30 a.m. nap. Breastfed to sleep then placed in her cot. Slept 45 mins. Woke up crying. 11 a.m. long breast feed. She dozed during the feed, but would not let me unlatch her and put her in her cot.

Afternoon Food taken. What time? Time, length and place of nap(s). How did you settle her? How long did it take?	12.30 vegetable casserole + pear purée. Enjoyed it. Ate 2 'ice cubes'-worth. 2 p.m. nap in the pram when out. Shopping. Slept 2½ hours. Woke happy. Breastfed when she woke up. 5 p.m. sweet potato and chicken + yoghurt. Ate well.
Evening routine Time started. Time she went into her cot. How did you settle her? Was she asleep or awake when placed into the cot? Evening awakenings?	Bath 6 p.m. Breastfed on my bed. Fell asleep at the breast. Asleep when put in her cot at 6.45. Woke 7.15, crying. Settled her in her cot by patting her. Took 15 mins.
During the night Times and length of waking. What did you do to resettle her?	Woke 11 p.m. Breastfed 5 mins. Fell asleep. Back into the cot. Same at 1 a.m. At 2.30 a.m. brought her to our bed. Fell asleep feeding. Fed again (in her sleep) at 3.45 a.m. and 5 a.m. At 6.15 woke and unable to resettle with a feed. Got up for the day.

What kind of a sleep problem does your baby have... and why?

Having kept a sleep diary, you may now have an inkling not only of the type of sleep problem that your baby has, but perhaps why she has it. As we have already seen, there is always a reason why a baby does not sleep well. In a newborn baby, it may be that her body clock has not yet adjusted into a mature pattern of more sleep being taken at night, or that she still needs very frequent feeds. In an older baby, however, a long-term sleep problem is likely to be down to behavioural or environmental factors. Remember, though, that all babies have occasional periods of poor sleep caused by teething pain, illness and so on.

It is useful at this point to look at some of the most common sleep problems and their possible causes.

Take a very honest look at what is happening around your baby's sleep. You may have a fantastic bedtime routine; you may have avoided ever bringing her into your bed; you may have never given her a dummy; and so forth. There may be *just one tiny thing* going wrong for you. (Continuing dawn feed? Rocking her to sleep at the start of the night? Lying beside her cot if she wakes during the night?) Unwittingly one of those small factors may be causing the misery of your broken nights. It can be very hard, when you are a loving, sensible and conscientious parent, to admit that there is something that you might be doing wrong around your baby's sleep, but you need to look very carefully at all of your routines.

There is no doubt at all that some babies are better sleepers than others. You might be a parent of more than one child and have never had problems with your older ones. Your bedtime routine with your sleepless baby may be just the same as it was with the others, so why are you having a problem now? The fact is that all babies are individual, and while, for example, falling asleep over a night-time bottle will not cause later waking problems for some babies, for others it is a recipe for night-time disaster.

You are about to change the way that you approach bedtime practices with your sleepless baby, but this does not mean that what you have been doing previously has been wrong. It is just that it may be *wrong for your baby right now.*

Don't forget, either, that some of the habits that you established to settle your newborn baby, which were appropriate at the time, may now be working against you. The prime example of this is continuing with night feeds when they are no longer nutritionally necessary.

Sleep problems and reasons

The problem	The possible reasons
My baby will not settle to sleep in her cot at night.	• She is getting too much or too little sleep during the day. • She doesn't like you to leave her alone. • There is a lack of a meaningful bedtime routine. • She is in the habit of falling asleep on the sofa/in the pram/in your bed.
My baby wakes during the night.	• It is normal for babies to wake in the night. Her problem is that she can't resettle without help. • She is too hot/cold/uncomfortable/ hungry or thirsty. • She is alarmed to wake and find herself in a different place from where she originally fell asleep. • She is unable to resettle without you feeding or rocking her back to sleep. • She has lost her dummy.
My baby wakes very early in the morning.	• She was over tired when she went to bed. • Her sleep skills are fragile, and this is the most difficult time for her to resettle alone. • She is accustomed to having a dawn feed or the ritual of getting into your bed. • The room is too light/ morning noises are disturbing her.
My baby feeds frequently during the night.	• She is hungry or thirsty. • She is feeding as a sleep trigger.
My baby will not settle for her daytime naps.	• She's not yet able to join her sleep cycles. • The naps are scheduled at the wrong times. • She is over tired.

Aiming for a goal

Once you have established the exact nature of your baby's sleep problem, you need to set goals as to what you want her sleep to be like. This is when you need to be realistic. While it is perfectly reasonable to expect your healthy six-month-old to settle by herself at the beginning of the night and sleep through for a solid 11–12 hours, expecting her to lie in until 9 a.m. on a weekend morning is clearly overly optimistic. Similarly, expecting your three-month-old baby to sleep through the night without a feed may be unrealistic, too.

When deciding what you would like to achieve for your baby's sleep, it may be useful for you to set some 'SMART' targets. These are targets that are:

- **Specific** – clear and unambiguous
- **Measurable** – you will know when you have reached it
- **Achievable** – you have the resources to reach it
- **Realistic** – you will be able to carry it out
- **Time related** – you are aiming for a specific deadline.

Here is an example:

- **Specific:** I want my baby to sleep without her dummy.
- **Measurable:** I will know that I have taught her this when she sleeps through the night without it.
- **Achievable:** I have the patience, resolve and knowledge to do this.
- **Realistic:** I know that her dependence on her dummy is merely a habit, and I can help wean her off this.
- **Time related:** I will start at the weekend and give myself a week to achieve this target.

Based on what you have learned so far, you might find it helpful to write a clear overview of your baby's sleep problem and what you would like to achieve. Use the example as a guide.

An overview of my baby's sleep

My baby's typical night's sleep is like this:	• She takes a long time to fall asleep at the beginning of the night. She will not go into her cot and needs to fall asleep on my bed with me close by. When she is asleep, I put her in her own cot, but she wakes up later, screaming. The only way to settle her is for her to come into my bed. She then sleeps all night with me, but she wriggles and kicks the covers off.
My baby is not sleeping through the night because:	• She can only fall asleep with me lying with her on my bed at the beginning of the night. • When she stirs later, she needs to come to my bed and for me to lie with her again.
What I want is for her to:	• be happy to fall asleep in her own cot at bedtime • sleep through the night in her cot.
To achieve this, I need to:	• teach her how to go to sleep happily in her cot at the start of the night • help her to learn that her cot is a safe and permanent place to sleep • break the ritual of her getting into my bed during the night.
I will know I have succeeded when:	• she is happy to go to sleep in her cot by herself • she sleeps through the night.

Getting motivated

By now you have established the exact nature of your baby's sleep problem and you are clear about your goal. You should also have a strong idea about how you intend to achieve that goal. The trouble is, though, that you are already exhausted and you feel a bit demoralized that, despite all your previous efforts in caring for your baby, you have a sleep problem on your hands.

In these circumstances, it can be very difficult to summon up the confidence and motivation needed for change.

You may find it useful to try the following two exercises:

1. Name three good things that will arise from improving your baby's sleep.
2. Name three things that you yourself have achieved over the past year.

Example

The three good things that will come from my baby sleeping through the night are:

1 She'll be better happier and less tearful.
2 I'll be able to join an evening yoga class.
3 She will nap better in the day.

Three things that I have achieved over the past year are:

1 I've had a baby.
2 I've decorated the spare bedroom.
3 I've given up smoking.

If you are still feeling unsure about tackling your baby's sleep problem, you should take an honest look at what is preventing you from starting. Once more, make a little list.

> **Example**
>
> The things that are holding me back from teaching my baby to sleep through the night are:
>
> 1 I'm scared of her crying. I don't believe that's right.
> 2 I like the contact with her during the night.
> 3 I'm worried that I might be too exhausted to carry it through.
> 4 Having my baby in bed with me means that I can avoid having sex with my partner.

Once you have been honest with yourself about what might be holding you back from teaching your baby to sleep, you will better placed to make a choice about whether you really want to sleep-train your baby and, if so, which method to choose.

If you decide to postpone tackling your baby's sleep plan, or if you plan to leave things as they are for the long term, then at least you can be sure in your own mind that you have made the decision.

This in itself can be very helpful because, for many people, to feel that their baby's behaviour is outside their control, or to have the vague sense that they ought to be addressing their baby's sleep behaviour but haven't, can be more unsettling than the sleep problem itself.

If you have decided that you really do want to commence sleep training, you need to start preparing to make the necessary changes.

Taking care of the practicalities... and caring for yourself

Before you begin sleep training, you need to do some simple forward planning:

1. If your baby is currently sleeping in bed with you, take some time to adjust mentally to the fact that she will soon be

sleeping in her own cot. However positive you might feel about the move, you may find that you have a small sense of regret, too. Make the most of your last few nights together, and check out your feelings. It may be that you can't wait for her to move out, but equally, despite the fact that her sleep and your own are disrupted, you fear that you will miss having her there. Remember that, even when she is sleeping in her own space, she can still be welcomed into your bed in the morning for a loving cuddle.

2. You will need to prepare any older brothers and sisters for the changes that you plan to make. Even the gentlest sleep training will involve some crying at night, and if older siblings are not used to hearing this, they may worry. Reassure them that you are teaching the little one how to sleep through the night. Explain that, when they hear her cries, you are awake and dealing with her. Older siblings may be disturbed by more than just night-time crying. Sometimes, it is necessary to leave an older child to his own devices as you tackle the settling problems of the younger one. Once again, you need to give as full an explanation as he can understand. After you have managed to settle the little one, you should turn your attention to your older one(s). Any sacrifices that they have made in terms of the loss of your attention or being disturbed during the night should be rewarded by your generous praise. This is especially important if your sleepless baby is sharing a room with an older sibling.

3. Similarly, if you have close neighbours, it's a good idea to inform them that you are about to teach your baby to sleep. They will appreciate the courtesy and are more likely to support you. Many times, sleep plans have had to be abandoned when parents fear disturbing or upsetting their neighbours. As with older children, if they are not used to hearing your child cry at night, they may fear that something

has happened to her or to you. If they understand the reason for your baby's cries, they are more likely to be able to ignore them.

4. Choose a period of relative quiet and stability in which to start sleep training. You are less likely to be able to stick with it if things are especially demanding at work, or if you are preparing for a family holiday, for instance. Although this might mean that you have to postpone changing your baby's sleep habits, it is better that you start later and achieve success. Even if just one of you is going to be largely responsible for the sleep training, you should check out what your partner's schedule is going to be like. Choose a time when your partner's support is more likely to be forthcoming. For most people, commencing a sleep training plan at the start of the weekend is an ideal time.

5. Getting support from your partner is so important when you start to change your baby's sleep behaviour. If you have a traditional set-up at home where one of you looks after the baby and the other one goes out to work, you may worry that your baby's crying will disturb your partner's sleep and make work the next day extremely difficult. Your partner may have a low tolerance of your baby's cries and see it as your responsibility to get up and stop the crying, regardless of the long-term implications of this. If your partner is like this, it might be helpful to suggest that they sleep in another room, if that is possible, for a short period. You also need to help them see that helping your baby to sleep will ultimately benefit all of you.

6. If you are in paid work, you should consider informing your boss and colleagues about what you are planning to do. They may not be able to decrease your workload, but they may be a little more understanding if you seem tired at work. Sharing

information about home (especially if it is about a baby) can often lead to warmer working relationships. Over the few nights of sleep training, you may value your colleagues' interest in how you are doing, as well as their advice and understanding.

7. Most important of all, you need to prepare yourself for the impact of sleep training your baby. Get as much support lined up as you can from friends, family and work colleagues. Asking a friend or relative to take the baby for a walk in the pram for a couple of hours during the day means that you can catch up on some precious missed sleep and will allow you to maintain your resolve for the coming night. Before you start, you need to get as much rest as you possibly can. Although evenings, after your baby has gone to bed, may be the only time that you can make phone calls or watch TV, you need to go to bed early for a few nights.

Ten things to remember

1. Don't let fear of things getting worse put you off improving your baby's sleep – they rarely do.
2. Even if things do get a bit worse, you are in control now and you will feel more positive.
3. Preparation is one of the keys to successful sleep training.
4. If you are to really help your baby sleep well, you need to be honest with yourself about all the issues around sleep.
5. Being honest with yourself doesn't mean being hard on yourself.
6. Don't blame yourself. You haven't got a sleep problem on your hands because you've been stupid, lazy or feckless!
7. Try not to compare how your baby sleeps with how others do.
8. Be clear about what you want to achieve when you are setting your goals.
9. Don't even think about attempting sleep training just because someone else has told you that you need to.
10. Remember that your baby does not sleep badly on purpose.

9

Taking control and helping your baby to sleep well

Now that you are armed with all the necessary information that you need about your baby's sleep and you have made all the possible preparations for change, it is time for you to take control and help him to sleep better. You may have been feeling a little out of control for a while, as you have struggled at night and at nap times. This feeling can be utterly demoralizing, especially if you are by nature an organized kind of person. For lots of people, who have been used to having control in their work and personal lives, the experience of becoming a parent can be a real shock.

Parenthood may not always fit the mental picture that you had in mind, and babies are not always the docile, smiling little beings that you might have imagined. You can take control over the many aspects of your baby's sleep, however, and what is more, he needs you to do this. Not just during sleep but in a world where he is vulnerable, your baby very much needs the security of knowing that Mummy or Daddy is in charge. Remember that he will not be able to improve his sleep without your help.

Choosing the method that will work for you

There are two main approaches which you should consider when sleep training your baby. Both, if consistently applied, will help your baby to sleep better.

The two *basic* sleep training methods are:

- **controlled crying** – leave your baby to cry himself to sleep from night 1, returning to reassure him briefly at specified intervals
- **gradual withdrawal** – remain with your baby as he learns to settle to sleep alone, and then gradually move away from him.

Controlled crying

Suitable for healthy babies of six months or more, and for parents who are able to allow their babies to cry themselves out. An especially useful method for families needing a very quick solution to their babies' sleep problems.

May not be suitable for babies who are under five months old, are unwell or have special needs. Not an acceptable method for parents who cannot bear to leave their babies to cry for long periods.

Gradual withdrawal

Suitable for babies of all ages. Especially good for those with ongoing medical or developmental difficulties. Will suit parents who cannot or will not allow their babies to cry excessively.

May not be suitable for parents in need of a speedy solution, or for those who are unable to commit to the demands of sitting beside their babies for lengthy periods during the night.

There are so many books available on babies' sleep, most of them claiming to have a new, fail-safe solution to all your problems. The truth is that all sleep training methods are variations on the two approaches above. It may be unrealistic to expect that one single method of sleep training will solve the problems of all babies. What works best for all babies is to identify the reason for waking and address this within the context of either of the two approaches.

Example

Your baby is in the habit of feeding himself to sleep at the beginning of the night. Because of this, he wakes several times during the night needing shorter feeds to resettle. He no longer requires night feeds for nutritional purposes but, instead, is feeding as a sleep cue.

Prepare

1. Introduce a consistent bedtime routine which will familiarize him with sleep cues other than just feeding.
2. Feed him after his bath, but do not allow him to fall asleep over the feed.
3. Before placing him in his cot, briefly look at a picture book together or have a spoken 'kiss goodnight' ritual. This will both ensure that he is awake when he goes down and will also break the close feed/sleep connection.
4. Choose your sleep training method.

Controlled crying

- **Night 1** After placing your awake baby in his cot, kiss him goodnight and then leave the room.
  - Leave him to cry for five minutes before returning briefly to him to pat, reassure and help to resettle him. Spend no more than a minute with him and then leave him again, even if he cries.
  - Leave it for ten minutes this time before returning and settling him very briefly again.
  - Extend the period of your absence to 15 minutes. Return to him if he is still crying and settle him briefly as before.
  - From then on, go in every 15 minutes until he has gone to sleep. Make sure that you are not in the room with him as he does this.
- **Night 2** After placing him in his cot awake, leave him and go in after ten minutes, then at five-minute intervals up to a

maximum of 20 minutes. If he is still awake and crying, go in to him and settle him in the same consistent manner every 20 minutes.

- **Night 3** Initially leave your baby for 15 minutes, then return at five-minute intervals to a maximum of 25 minutes. After tonight, he should be sleeping through the night of your absence. You should continue to go in frequently throughout the period that your baby is crying hard.

Top tips: Andrea Grace's gentler take on controlled crying

I have noticed that what babies find most upsetting about the controlled crying method is being comforted almost to the point of sleep and then being left alone again. For this reason, I tend to recommend to my families that if they undertake controlled crying they adopt a slightly different approach to the classic one described above.

I advise that parents go in to their babies very frequently but for the briefest possible time. Ideally, during the period of distressed crying the parent should go in every 1–3 minutes but for no more than a few seconds. The idea is that baby knows that he has not been abandoned and he learns how to self-settle. There is no need to gradually extend the period of your absence. You should continue to go in frequently throughout the period that your baby is crying hard.

Using this method, it is perfectly all right to speak lovingly to your baby: 'Shh, good boy in your cot!' You can kiss him and reposition him but that is all. No picking up or feeding again and no rocking, patting or stroking. If you try to soothe him and stop the crying, he will be all the more upset when you leave him.

Act in your normal loving way, bustling in and out to fold a towel or put something away in a drawer. Babies find it distressing when parents avoid speech and eye contact with them, so if you have been advised to do this – please ignore it!

As soon as your baby's cries turn to merely fussing, or become softer and have a rhythmic, tuneful quality, you should not go in to him, even if you are due to. He is getting himself off to sleep now, and your going in will only interfere with the process. Neither should you go in if he is awake but quiet.

As with any form of sleep training, *this method will only work if you start it when you first put your baby to bed.*

Gradual withdrawal method

- **Step 1** (approximately two nights) Place your baby in his cot while he is awake and remain beside him until he has gone to sleep. You can give as much physical contact as he needs to settle – leaning right into his cot if necessary – but it is best not to take him out of the cot or feed him again. He will cry because he is used to being fed to sleep, but don't worry: you are constantly beside him to reassure him and to make sure that he comes to no harm.
- **Step 2** (approximately two nights) Once your baby becomes comfortable about falling asleep in his cot and is no longer dependent on sucking or being rocked to sleep, you need to withdraw some of your physical contact but not leave him alone yet. Remain beside his cot and make sure that, as he enters sleep, you are not touching him.
- **Step 3** (up to two weeks) Move your chair a little farther away from your baby's cot each night until you are outside his room. Do this in tiny stages, so that your baby has time to get used to the change.

Insight

Do you want a gentle solution that works within a week?

There is no reason why you can't combine the two methods. Start of with the first two stages of the gradual withdrawal method and then move on to Night 1 of the controlled crying method.

Important points:

- Sleep training should always commence when you first put your baby to bed at night. Allowing him to fall asleep in your arms or over a feed at the beginning of the night and then starting the training when he first wakes up will be too confusing and difficult for him.
- When you resettle your baby during the night, use the same approach as you did at the beginning of the night – for example, going in at two- to five-minute intervals if you are using the controlled crying method, or returning to sit beside him if you are using the gradual withdrawal method.

Top tip

Based on the knowledge that you have of your baby, understanding the reason for his sleep difficulty and knowing your own strengths and limitations, you can design a sleep plan that is individually tailored to his needs and those of your family.

Throughout this book, we have tended to look at the gradual withdrawal approach, as this is safe for all and effective, provided that it is carried out in a consistent manner and followed through to its conclusion – ultimately, you have to leave your child to settle to sleep alone.

Whether you decide on a 'controlled crying' technique or a 'gradual withdrawal' one will depend on your values as a parent, your family circumstances and your level of desperation. Remember that the decision is yours, and whatever choice you make, your success with it will depend on how consistent you are and your ability to see it through. So make sure that you choose an approach with which you feel not only confident but comfortable.

Designing your baby's sleep plan

Now that you have identified the *reason* for your baby's sleep difficulties, and chosen a *method* of sleep training with which you feel happy, have decided on a *time* when you are able to start, and have informed those people who are likely to be affected by it, it is time to get on and design your sleep plan.

It is best to have something written down, as this will remind you of what you are meant to be doing. Writing your plan will give it clarity and help to focus your thoughts. Remember that simple is best. You might like to design your own sleep plan or try something like the sleep action plan here.

Sleep action plan (nights 1 and 2)

Action plan	Night 1 What happened	Night 2 What happened
At the start of the night Introduce a very consistent bedtime routine, when I know that he is beginning to get sleepy but is not overtired. Take him directly to his room after his bath and prepare him for bed. Give him milk sitting in the armchair and then read a storybook with him. If he protests about any of these changes, I need to remain calm and in control.	He liked the new bedtime routine but was very lively when I put him in his cot. It took him 55 minutes from cot to sleep. Not much crying at first. More playful really. Fell asleep at 8.25. Woke at 9.15. Settled very easily and quickly by me patting him in his cot.	When I put him into the cot, he was playful again. I pottered in and out of the room until he started 'fussing' and was ready to sleep. Then sat beside him like last night. Took 20 minutes for him to go to sleep. Not much crying.
After the story, put him in the cot while he is awake. I know that he is going to cry, so I will stay beside him for as long as it takes until he falls asleep. This way, although he might be angry and frustrated, I know that he will not be afraid. When he is asleep, I will go to bed early, so that I can respond consistently and calmly to him when he wakes later.		

(Continued)

Action plan	Night 1 What happened	Night 2 What happened
During the night When he wakes up during the night, sit beside him until he goes back to sleep. I know that this will take some time and there will be more crying, and I will be prepared for this to happen. No matter how many times he wakes up, or how long he is awake for, I am resolved to keep him in his cot.	Woke at 12.30. Very difficult to resettle. Awake on and off until 2.20. I felt very desperate but stuck with it. Woke again at 4.15. Took approx. half an hour to resettle.	Woke at 12.45. Settled within 15 minutes of me patting him.
Early in the morning Keep him in his cot until 7 a.m., even if he wakes earlier than this. If I bring him into my bed at dawn and allow him to go back to sleep, it will make all that we have achieved earlier meaningless.	Woke again at 6.15. Would normally have got him up at this time, but stayed with him until he fell back to sleep at 6.50. Woke again at 7.20 and got him up for the day.	Didn't wake again until 6.30! He was completely wide awake and smiling, and as he had had such a good night, I decided to get him up for the day.
During the day I am going to aim for two naps and let him fall asleep in whatever way is most comfortable for him. Once he has learned good night-time sleep skills, I will help him to improve his daytime sleep skills too.	9.45 a.m. he looked tired, so I put him in his cot. Cried for half an hour before eventually settling. Slept for 30 mins. Woke up still looking tired – couldn't bear to let him cry again so got him up. 1.45 p.m. looking tired again. Went out in the pushchair and he slept for two hours. Woke up happy.	Waited until 10 a.m. before putting him into his cot for a nap. Cried again, like yesterday for half an hour – even though I was next to him. Slept for 1½ hours, though, and woke up happy. Enjoyed his lunch. 45 mins at 3 p.m. this afternoon in his pushchair.

Sleep action plan (nights 3–7)

	Night 3 *What happened*	Night 4 *What happened*	Night 5 *What happened*	Night 6 *What happened*	Night 7 *What happened*
At the start of the night As before, but begin to move away from him as he goes to sleep.	Sat next to the cot but no patting. Fell asleep in 15 mins.	Moved my chair farther away from the cot. Closed my eyes and did some yoga breathing – so wasn't watching him – 10 mins to settle.	Chair even farther away. Took him 15 mins to settle. No crying.	Chair positioned almost at his door. Took him 5 mins to settle. No crying.	Left the room to wash my hands, and when I came back, he was asleep!
During the night Leave him for a few moments before going to him, to see if he can settle himself.	Woke 1 a.m. Went to settle him but he was already asleep.	Think I heard him stir a couple of times, but no need to get up to him.	Didn't wake during the night.	Didn't wake during the night.	Didn't wake during the night.
Early in the morning As above.	Woke 4 a.m. Took an hour to resettle him. Woke 6 a.m. Too tired to get up to him again. By time I'd summoned the energy he'd gone back to sleep.	Woke 7.10 a.m.!	Woke 6.45 a.m. Got him up for the day.	Woke 6.30 a.m. Heard him chatting to himself so didn't go in. Eventually he called for me at 7.15 a.m.	As yesterday.
During the day We are both finding these hard. I will aim for one nap in his cot and one in his pushchair.	Put him into his cot at 9.15. Stayed with him. Cried for 20 mins. Slept 1 hour. Afternoon nap (45 mins) in pushchair.	Into his cot at 9.30. Stayed with him. Cried for 10 mins. Slept 1 hour 15 mins. Afternoon nap (1 hour) in pushchair.	Put in cot at 9.20. Left him as needed to answer the phone. Cried for 5 mins. Slept 1 hour. Afternoon nap (45 mins) in pushchair.	Cot at 9.15. Left him. Cried 10 mins but not too severe. Slept 1 hour. Cot again for afternoon nap. Left him as this morning. Slept 1 hour.	Cot: 9.30–11 a.m. Cot: 2.30–3.30 p.m. Both times, put in his cot and left to settle

Once you have designed your sleep plan, it is advisable for you to show it to a person whom you trust. This is so that they know what you are planning to do and will be better able to support you during the process. Another person will also be able to tell you if there any obvious errors in your plan.

Making it work

By now, you know why your child is not sleeping through the night, what you need to do to solve his sleep problem and how to do it.

Once you have made the decision to start changing your baby's sleep habits, you need demonstrate the three Cs:

- consistency
- calmness
- confidence.

These three qualities will make the process easier for both you and your baby. There may be times when your resolve weakens, and you need to be prepared for these.

If you possibly can, you should seek out someone to support you during this process. Practical help, such as taking your baby for a long walk during the day to allow you to catch up on some rest, is absolutely invaluable and will keep you going. If you have been up for hours in the middle of the night, things will not look so bleak if you know that you will get a two-hour nap the following day.

Sometimes, all you need is some moral support: someone telling you that you are doing a good job and listening to you when you describe how the sleep training is going.

Sleep training stumbling blocks

The problem	The solution
After crying for a period, my baby vomits.	Quickly and calmly clean him up, and then place him back in the cot with no further feeding and carry on sleep training. If necessary, stay beside him but do not pick him out of his cot unless he is sick again.
He wakes his older sibling(s) with his cries.	Explain to them (if they are old enough to understand) that he is learning how to sleep at night and that you are awake and looking after him. Be aware that the disruption to other family members' sleep is short term and that, if you stick with the training, all of you will benefit. Remain calm and confident.
He cries for much longer than I expected/his crying is very severe.	Don't be frightened of his crying. As long as you are close beside him or returning to him periodically, he will know that he has not been abandoned. He is crying out of frustration at the change in your usual response to him.
Part way through the sleep training, he has developed a cold, bout of teething, etc.	Take care of his physical discomfort by lifting him from the cot, but keeping him in his room. Give a drink of water and a dose of infant painkiller if needed. Hold him in your arms if necessary for around 20 minutes, until the painkiller has worked and he feels more settled. Then place him back in his cot and carry on where you left off.

This help doesn't have to come from a partner. It can come from a friend, mother or sister, for instance. Your health visitor should be able to offer you some advice and moral support as well as putting you in touch with other parents who might share the same issues. It helps if you are living in an area where nearby there are other parents with babies and you are able to support one another. If you are alone in your area with a baby or young family you might find it helpful to explore some social media groups, where parents from all over the world are able to establish a supportive network.

How long will it take?

During most forms of sleep training, you can expect things to be a bit worse for up to a week before they begin to improve. If you plan for the worst, it will be easier to cope when things are difficult.

- Try to avoid planning any special events when you know that you are going to be sleep training your baby.
- Stock up the freezer and cupboards with easy meals for both the family and your baby a week or so before you begin.
- Abandon all unnecessary housework. Let the ironing pile up and cope with it when you have more energy.
- Learn how to 'power nap' – that is, always rest if you can when your baby is sleeping during the day.
- Try not to spend all day in the house alone with your baby. Even though you are tired, it will do you both good to go out for a walk or to an organized baby activity at least once a day.
- If you are working, try to take a couple of days of annual leave, but still send your child to his usual daycare provider... and don't feel guilty about spending that time resting.

A word about naps and timing

If your baby tends to sleep a lot during the evening or late afternoon and has a very late bedtime, you should aim to bring his bedtime forward in gradual stages of around 15 minutes each night before you begin sleep training. This is so that his body clock has time to adjust to an earlier bedtime. You will, of course, need to address the timing of his daytime naps for this.

It may be that you can abandon a late afternoon or teatime nap altogether and then simply introduce an earlier bedtime. If it is impossible to drop that late nap, you may find that you have to cut the duration of it by ten minutes or so each day and then systematically bring his bedtime forward by the same amount. If you suddenly bring his bedtime forward from, say, 11 p.m. to 7 p.m., you'll find yourself in real difficulty and sleep training will be particularly tough for him, as his body may simply not be ready for sleep at a much earlier time.

Another thing about naps is that, for many babies, the old adage that 'sleep begets sleep' holds true. The better rested your baby is at bedtime, the less likely he is to struggle to sleep through overtiredness at bedtime. It is typically from around 18 months old that babies' over-napping during the day can cause settling difficulties at night.

Evaluating your success and getting the support you need

Once you have started helping your baby to improve their sleep, you may find it helpful to evaluate your progress as you go. Sometimes, if things seem to be dragging on, it can be useful to check out how far you have come and what you are still aiming for. This will show you what improvements you have made and help you to keep motivated. It will also help you identify what, if anything, might be going wrong.

Every morning ask yourself the following questions:

1. What was good about his sleep last night?
2. What was bad about his sleep last night?
3. How far did I stick to the sleep plan?
4. What am I going to do tonight?

Example

1 **What was good about his sleep last night?**
   He went to sleep in his own cot without me rocking or feeding him to sleep. He didn't wake up during the evening, as he usually does.

2 **What was bad about last night?**
   He woke up at 2 a.m. and took an hour to resettle. Normally, he would have gone straight back to sleep if I'd brought him into bed with me.

3 **How far did I stick to the sleep plan?**
   I stuck to it completely!

4 **What am I going to do tonight?**
   I am going to continue to teach him that his cot is a safe and permanent place. The more I reinforce this, the more the message will get home to him, and he will soon stop waking during the night.

When you evaluate your progress, you will need to keep your original goal in the forefront of your mind. Remind yourself of the advantages of what his good sleep will bring, not only for him, but for you and the rest of the family, too.

Top tip
You should try to stick to your sleep plan for at least three nights. If at the end of this time you have made no progress at all, you should consider adopting a different approach.

What if your sleep plan hasn't worked?

You might have started a sleep plan with utter resolve and confidence. Your goals may have been clear and your plan utterly watertight, but somehow your baby just didn't respond as he was meant to and you are left exhausted and asking yourself, 'Where did I go wrong?'

If sleep training has not worked/is not working for you, it is down to one or more of the following reasons:

- **The method is at odds with your natural, instinctive parenting style**. This means that your heart isn't really in it, and you need to consider the following:
  - whether to try a different, gentler or tougher approach
  - whether a part of you enjoys and allows contact with your baby during the night – if so, that's OK. Give yourself permission to enjoy the closeness with him during the night.
- **You have lost heart when progress has not been quick enough**. If this is the case, you should consider speeding up the process by allowing your baby to cry it out. After a period of preparation such as establishing a consistent bedtime routine and teaching him how to go to sleep aware that he is in his cot, this method will be less traumatic than if you had started it from scratch. It should be quicker, too.
- **Your baby has been distressed by the process of sleep training**. You should not give up, but switch to a gentler method. 'OK, I can't leave him alone to cry, but I can at least teach him how to go to sleep in his own bed.' Remaining close beside him as he makes changes to his sleep behaviour and then withdrawing in small gradual stages will work better for you.
- **Circumstances such as an illness, holiday or house move have broken the consistency that is needed for success**. These events of family life are usually outside of our control and can have a real impact on our babies' sleep. The best that you can do is to put sleep training 'on ice' and try not to lose any ground that you might have gained. For instance, if you have been making progress and your baby suddenly goes through a bad phase of teething, there is no reason to reintroduce night feeds or bring him into your bed again. It is better to comfort him in his room, with a cuddle, a drink

of water and a dose of infant painkiller. Once he is calm and comfortable, you should resettle him in his cot. This kind of approach will give him the attention and contact that he needs when he is unwell, while not allowing him to lose the ground that he has gained.

- **You have been criticized by others for your approach.** While up to a point it is good to listen to others' advice and to appreciate their concern for you and your baby, it is ultimately your choice as his parent to care for him as you see fit. You know your own baby better than anyone else and you also know your own limitations and capabilities. Thank them for their advice, tell them that your baby's needs are your top priority and that you feel you are meeting them in the best possible way. Of course, this is particularly difficult if the criticism is coming from your partner. If this is the case, you need to take the time to discuss what approach will not only benefit your baby but also be acceptable to both of you.

- **You have suddenly brought his bedtime forward by several hours before his body has had time to adjust.** If your baby is used to a late bedtime, suddenly changing this will inevitably bring problems, as he may simply not be 'programmed' to sleep at an earlier time. You can tackle this by gradually bringing his bedtime forward by ten minutes each evening before or even during sleep training. There is an alternative: if your baby takes a late nap at, say, 6 p.m., you can start his bedtime routine then and put him down for the night after this. In other words, you substitute his nap time for his bedtime. Provided that you observe the golden rule of his being awake when he is placed in his cot, you should subsequently be able to resettle him there if he stirs. A word of warning, though: be prepared for him to wake up earlier in the morning if he has gone to bed early the night before. When you first start sleep training, success means having your baby sleep for a 10- to 11-hour night-time stretch.

- **You have not followed the method to its conclusion.** It is not at all uncommon to commence sleep training, achieve a degree of success and then get stuck. This is particularly the case with the gentler methods. What tends to happen is that you teach your baby to fall asleep in his cot with you sitting beside him. This may work very well at first, but when you come to try and leave the room, you may encounter some problems. This is because he has figured out that, when he wakes up, he will find that you are no longer beside him. This leads to his developing the sleep like that of a 'guard dog' – that is, he is reluctant to settle to sleep and will delay giving in to sleep for as long as he can. He may also resist settling into deep sleep and be fitful and easily roused, especially during the evening. To make progress, you may have to force the pace a bit and withdraw from the room before he has gone to sleep. There will, of course, be protest and/or crying, in which case you will need to return at frequent intervals to reassure him. You need, though, to make sure that, when he does eventually give in to sleep, you are not beside him. If you can do this, you will improve his chances of sleeping the whole way through the night.

- **You have started following the sleep plan at the first or subsequent waking rather than at the beginning of the night.** It is absolutely vital that, when you decide to start sleep training, you concentrate first and foremost on how your baby settles at the beginning of the night, even though you may not have any difficulty in getting him off to sleep at bed time. If you allow him to fall asleep over his feed, in your arms, downstairs on the sofa or in your bed, only to later transfer him into his cot, he will naturally wake up later feeling alarmed. He will need you to recreate the circumstances under which he originally fell asleep at the start of the night. Not only this, but having had the equivalent of a 'power nap', he will find it especially difficult to fall asleep again without your help. Try to capitalize on the fact that at the very start of the night he is surrounded by night-time sleep prompts and is sleepy.

Sometimes, if you are failing to make progress with sleep training, you may need to have a rethink and change your approach. While a consistent approach is usually recommended during sleep training, if things really are not going well, you may have to switch tactics.

> When Polly was eight months old, we found that her night-time sleeping was getting worse instead of better. We decided that we needed to take action and sleep train her. Neither of us liked the idea of her crying herself to sleep, so we decided to use a more gradual approach.
>
> We decided that, first of all, we would help her to go to sleep without me breastfeeding her. First, I would feed her and then take her off the breast while she was still awake and then rock her in my arms until she went to sleep. After this, I was going to cut down on the amount of rocking and place her in the cot while she was awake and comfort her there until she went to sleep. We were going to start with just the beginning of the night first and continue to feed her to sleep and bring her into bed with us when she woke up in the middle of the night. Once she was settling well at the start of the night, we were going to tackle her waking up during the night.
>
> We were very positive when we started and she did make some progress. She woke much later in the night, for instance. To be honest, though, we never really got beyond square one, as the commitment of all that sitting beside the cot was just too much for us. I think it might have been confusing for Polly, too. I know that we needed to move on to addressing the night feeds, but we were shattered and the whole thing was dragging on for too long. After sitting down and taking an honest look at what we were doing, we decided that it was in all our interests to implement a shorter and more clearly structured sleep plan. We decided to do the thing that we both had originally been against – to let her cry it out.

The work that we had done in establishing a good bedtime routine and helping her to settle in her cot at the start of the night was not wasted. She was happy to settle in her cot, but now we had to put her into her cot and go!

We returned to her every two minutes when she was crying and went in every 15 minutes after that to reassure her (and ourselves) that everything was all right. It took her 45 minutes the first time we did it. She woke up just once towards dawn and this time it took her 25 minutes to resettle. She then woke up at 7.30 a.m. I was almost afraid to get her out of her cot as I thought she would hate me. She was fine, though, full of smiles and totally her normal self.

On the second night, she cried for just ten minutes and then slept through until 5 a.m. I heard her cry and was getting ready to go and reassure her, but found when I got to her room that she had gone back to sleep by herself.

By the third night, she went to her cot and 'fussed' for a few minutes before settling herself to sleep. We didn't need to go back to her at all. She then slept through the night, and we woke up to her 'chatting' at 7.15 the next morning.

Letting her cry it out turned out to be the best solution for us in the end, even though we had been against it originally. It was not easy to listen to her crying, and I'm glad that we started off with a gentler approach as I think this helped with the process. All in all, I think that sleep training was one of the best things that we have done for her.

Sometimes things work out in the opposite way, which illustrates that, on some occasions, sticking to the plan for three nights might not be a sensible option:

Jonah was a year old when we decided that we needed to do something about his frequent night waking. There was no reason that we could think of why he was waking up so often during the night, except that it was habit and he was used to one of us rocking him to sleep at the start of the night and then repeating this again later, sometimes as many as four times! He was a strong, healthy boy, and we were advised that the best way to teach him how to sleep was to do 'controlled crying'. This method had worked for lots of my friends, and I presumed it was the one and only way to teach him how to sleep through. I'll be honest that I wasn't looking forward to it much, but I thought that it would really benefit him and it would be quick.

The first night we tried it was absolutely awful. We planned to return to him every five minutes, then ten minutes and then at 15-minute intervals, but after 20 minutes he was sick all over his clothes and his cot. We were told that this might happen, so we changed him as best as we could and then put him back in his cot. He was sick again after another ten minutes or so, and we cleaned him again. At this time, it was very difficult for us to remain resolved, but somehow we managed to stick with it, and he eventually fell asleep sobbing after nearly two hours.

To be fair, he did sleep better than he had ever done before on that night, but I think this was because he was completely exhausted. I couldn't sleep at all because I felt so guilty.

On the following night, Jonah was sick as I moved to put him in his cot. As far as I was concerned, enough was enough. This was clearly not the right approach for him.

We abandoned the whole thing and went back to our previous settling techniques of rocking him to sleep. Even this began to take longer than it used to do. He was still waking during the night and needing to be rocked again.

After a while, we sought help from a sleep specialist, who recommended a more gradual transition from being rocked to sleep to settling in his cot alone. It involved us placing him in his cot and then staying close beside him but not rocking him to sleep. We were to withdraw a little farther from him at night-time only when he was comfortable. We felt that this was a better solution for Jonah, even though it demanded more in terms of time commitment from us.

Gradually withdrawing from Jonah at the start of the night took three weeks rather than three nights, but we got there in the end. He now sleeps the whole way through the night. He did not vomit during this second kind of sleep training, and although we were very tired during it, we felt it was the best thing for him.

Ten things to remember

1. It is important to choose a sleep training method that matches your parenting style.
2. No matter how gentle a solution you choose, you should be prepared for your baby to cry.
3. Despite the number of books on babies and sleep available, there are just two training methods.
4. Understanding why your baby is waking and crying is the key to gentle sleep training.
5. Writing down your sleep plan will give you focus and clarity.
6. When you start sleep training, your baby needs you to be calm, confident and consistent.
7. Be prepared for things to go wrong and don't be discouraged if they do.
8. Accept that, when your baby's sleep improves, it's down to your intervention – not coincidence.
9. If things are not progressing, you need to make a confident decision – give it longer? Change your approach?
10. Be honest with yourself when it comes to evaluating your progress.

10

Keeping on the right track

Once you have invested so much time and effort in teaching your baby to sleep through the night, you need to make sure that you do not let things slip back again. You really don't want to go through the process again, do you? What's more, your baby doesn't want to go through it again, either.

Most babies will need just a few nights of sleep training before their problem is solved and they never look back, sleeping 12 hours a night and taking regular restorative daytime naps as necessary for the rest of their babyhood. Some, however, have more fragile sleep skills than others, and for these babies, sleep will always be a little problematic. These are the babies whose sleep goes awry at the slightest change, such as a holiday, illness, house move and so on.

If your child is one of these, then you need to be extra attentive to her sleep needs and be very wary of allowing unhelpful habits to develop again.

All babies will have the odd bad night, and it is unrealistic to expect that, once you have taught her how to sleep through the night, you will never be up with her in the small hours again. You need to be aware that, when she is genuinely unwell, it might be necessary to comfort her in your arms for as long as she needs you to during the night. As soon as she is better, however, you need to allow her to carry on sleeping as she did before the illness.

Insight

It usually takes two or three consecutive nights of her coming into your bed, being given night feeds or being rocked to sleep, for instance, for this behaviour to become a habit again.

Going on holiday

It is a real shame that many parents dread the thought of going away on holiday, in case it disrupts their baby's sleep or causes problems on returning home. No one feels comfortable about letting their baby cry while they are staying in a hotel, tent, caravan or holiday cottage. Not only is this disruptive for the family, but it can also upset other nearby holidaymakers.

It is far better, when you are away, to be a little flexible with your baby's sleep routine. She is likely to sleep for longer during the daytime if she is out in the open air in her pram or being carried around in a backpack. If this is the case, allow her to go to bed much later. If she wants to stay up with you while you have dinner, this is absolutely all right and it is not at all necessary to keep to her normal bedtime if this doesn't suit you on holiday.

When you do put her to bed for the night, however, try to use some of the sleep triggers which she is used to at home. These include the same songs that you sing around bedtime, her goodnight storybook, her familiar sleep suit and her usual teddy/blanket/comforter. It might not be possible to bath her every night, but you can still use your same bath-time song as you wash her hands, face and bottom, and clean her teeth.

Even if her cot is very close to your bed, it is better that you continue to settle her there rather than under the covers with you. Not only will this prevent her resisting going in her cot when she returns home, but it will enable you all to have better nights' sleep when you are on holiday, too.

Travelling

Babies' sleep is often seriously disrupted by travelling – especially long distances. If your baby is like most and tends to be lulled to sleep with motion, then she is likely to sleep on and off during any journey. Of course, if you have travelled during the day, this excessive sleep can affect her ability to settle down and sleep at night once you have reached your destination. Her settling can, of course, be further affected by the fact that she will be sleeping in a different environment from home.

There are two possible solutions to this one:

1. Travel during the night.
2. If you travel during the day and she has slept a lot on the way, put her to bed much later than usual, and only then when she is showing signs of tiredness. She is far less likely to struggle to settle if you do this and you will avoid all the negative sleep associations and habits which can occasionally develop in relation to a holiday cot.

Plane journeys

If you are intending to travel by plane or if you are going to a country which has a significant time difference, it is worth planning ahead so that you can minimize any disruption to your baby's (and your) sleep.

1. Reserve a bassinet for your baby to sleep in during the journey, or find out the policy on taking baby car seats on board.
2. Take an infant painkiller on board, in case she needs it for earache on take-off or, especially, descent.
3. If you do take a painkiller, fresh, unopened sachets are easier to use and have the advantage of being pre-measured.
4. If your baby is old enough, buy some dried organic apple rings. Hook one on to her thumb and allow her to suck and chew it if she gets bored. This will also help with her ear

pressure. Alternatively, use a dummy or offer a breast feed, or a drink from a bottle or cup.

5. Dress your baby in a simple one-piece soft suit with popper fastenings and take two or three more with you for the journey. These should double up as pyjamas.

6. Try not to check in her pram until you are about to board. This way she should be able to nap in it if she needs to as you wait for the flight.

7. Check in as early as you can, and don't be afraid to ask if there are any spare seats. They may give you an extra one so that you have more space for your baby and your stuff. Remember that it is in the airline's own interests that you make sure that you are comfortable. That way, fewer passengers will be disturbed.

8. As soon as you can after take-off, offer your baby a drink. This will help to ease any pressure in her ears and prevent dehydration.

9. Allow your baby to sleep as much as she likes on the plane. The motion may help her sleep for longer than normal, and you should encourage this.

10. Regardless of the time difference, feed her at her usual times as far as possible. If you need a bottle to be warmed, ask well in advance. The cabin crew might be busy or might make the bottle too hot, in which case you will have to wait for it to cool down.

11. When your baby is awake, entertain her by walking her up and down, showing her the in-flight film and allowing her to play with a few safe objects. Don't bother packing too many toys. She'll soon get bored with them.

12. Once at your destination, if she is awake, allow her time to familiarize herself with her new surroundings. Then when she is looking tired, use all the familiar verbal sleep cues in your preparation for bed.

13. Do not allow another (especially unfamiliar) family member to put her to bed on her first night – no matter how tempting that might be.

14. Try to go to bed at the same time as your baby, and if you are travelling with your partner, you might like to organize yourselves into shifts to deal with the night or very early morning waking which is so common when you change time zones.

15. It is likely that your baby will adjust to the time change quicker than you will. To encourage this, allow her to sleep freely during the early part of the following day, but then restrict afternoon and tea-time naps, so that she is tired at her new evening bedtime. If you need to put your baby to bed later than usual, you should do so, rather than putting her to bed at a time when she is simply not tired and possibly creating a negative sleep association with the new cot.

16. Exposure to daylight is the best way to help your baby to adapt to a new time zone.

Moving house

Moving house can be exciting and stressful; it can also be exhausting, especially if you are caring for a baby as well. It is easy to overlook your baby's sleep needs when you are busy ferrying furniture to and fro and sorting out rooms. Here are some simple tips to help you cope.

- Try to sort out first the place where your baby will be sleeping, so that you have somewhere to settle her for a nap when she needs it.
- Take a few familiar objects from her old room, so that she feels a sense of security.
- If she has napped a lot during the day, be prepared to put her to bed later than usual, so that she finds it easier to sleep. It would be a shame if her first experience of her new sleeping environment was lying awake and struggling to settle.

- Keep as many elements from her usual bedtime routine as possible. If you are accustomed to using verbal sleep prompts such as songs and stories as part of your routine, this should be easy for you as these elements are utterly portable.
- Do not bring her into bed with you even if you are very tired and need sleep. If you do this, she will get the message that, in the new home, she sleeps with Mummy and Daddy!

A new baby in the family

When you are expecting another baby, it is wise to make sure that your older toddler is sleeping through the night in her own cot or bed. The last thing that you want to do is to evict your precious older one from your bedroom to make room for the little one.

Presuming that you have already done this, you need to make sure that you maintain her independence, while continuing to reassure her that she is still your special girl. The following suggestions might help you achieve this.

- A few days before your new baby is due, have the Moses basket ready, next to your bed, so that your toddler is able to understand that that is where her new brother or sister will be sleeping. This way, it will not come as quite such a surprise when the baby comes home.
- When she first sees the new baby, whether in the hospital or at home, make sure that your arms are free for her. Allow her to look into the crib in her own time and, as well as giving her the chance to see the new baby, have a special gift in the crib just for her.
- When you first come home, you need to follow your older child's normal routine as much as possible. Newborn babies are pretty flexible (certainly more so than toddlers), and if you need to put the little one down for a moment to attend to your big girl, the baby will come to no harm.

- Try if you can to continue to put your toddler to bed as usual. You might need to do this with a baby in your arms, but the main focus of attention should be on the older one.
- It is not possible to tell your toddler too much just how much you love her. She really needs to hear this when a little one has just come into her life.
- Try not to worry about your new baby crying and waking your older one. Toddlers are surprisingly good at ignoring night-time cries. Part of the reason for this is that they know it is not their problem.

Your own sleep needs

Many parents are shocked to find that, after teaching their baby to sleep through the night, they have somehow lost the ability to sleep themselves.

This is not surprising; after several weeks or months of deeply disturbed sleep, it can be difficult to regain a good sleep pattern. If you cast your mind back to how the sleep cycles work, you will recall that babies tend to wake up as they are coming into a light sleep phase. Their waking is natural and therefore not too damaging. You, on the other hand, may have been used to being woken during the deep phase of a sleep cycle, and after a time this disturbance can be very debilitating. You may have responded by not allowing yourself to relax fully into sleep, knowing that you are soon going to be woken up… and so you now have a sleep problem. Don't worry. If you were a good sleeper before you had children, there is every chance that you can be a good sleeper again.

1. Start a relaxing, repetitive bedtime routine for yourself. Seriously, you will benefit from the sleep cues just as much as your baby has.

2. Go to bed at a reasonable time – that is, do not allow yourself to become overtired.

3. Avoid caffeine-containing drinks in the afternoon and evening.

4. If you can't relax and go to sleep, read a book. You may not be asleep, but your body will still be resting.

5. If, when you turn off the light, you struggle to go to sleep, close your eyes and make an alphabetical list of, for instance, countries, birds or parts of the body. This might sound silly, but these mental exercises prevent your mind from wandering, excessive planning or worrying. They provide a focus and yet are sufficiently unimportant as to not prevent you from sleeping. If you do these regularly, they will begin to act as a sleep prompt for you.

6. If you do have something that is on your mind, allow yourself 15 minutes of planning or 'worry time'. This is all you need as, after that, your thoughts will just be going around in circles. After the 15 minutes, you should either get back to making your lists or get up, have a warm drink and then return to bed once you are feeling tired.

7. Be reassured that good sleep will come back if you relax and give it time.

Enjoying the fruits of your success

If you have successfully treated your baby's sleep problem, you should give yourself a massive pat on the back. You alone know that, although it can be a straightforward process, it is certainly not easy. Take a moment to think of your unique skills and qualities and what you have achieved.

Ten things to remember

1. You have cared enough about your baby to want to help her.
2. You have watched and assessed her in a way that only you could have done.
3. You have read and listened to information to equip yourself with the tools to help her.
4. You have taken that information and designed (whether formally or not) a sleep plan for her.
5. You have put that plan into practice – even though it might have been easier to give in at times.
6. You have shown patience and compassion while she has struggled to learn how to sleep.
7. You have allowed her to learn independent sleep skills, even when you have wanted to run to her and cuddle her to sleep.
8. You have taken control and improved your own confidence as a parent.
9. You have taught your baby a vital life-skill: the ability to enjoy sleep and all its benefits.
10. You have given your baby a most precious gift. Well done.

Further help and resources

Council for Disabled Children
Umbrella body for the disabled children's sector bringing together professionals, practitioners and policy-makers.
Website: councilfordisabledchildren.org

Association of Breastfeeding Mothers
Voluntary organization providing support from mother to mother. Telephone and email counselling.
Website: www.abm.me.uk Email: admin@abm.me.uk Tel: +44 (0)844 412 2948
National Breastfeeding Helpline: +44 (0)3003 305 453

The Lullaby Trust
The Lullaby Trust raises awareness of sudden infant death syndrome (SIDS), provides expert advice on safer sleep for babies and offers emotional support for bereaved families.
Website: www.lullabytrust.org.uk

Childcare.co.uk
Social network resource to help parents find childcare and other child-related facilities in their area.
Website: www.childcare.co.uk

Cry-sis
Offers support for families with excessively crying, sleepless and demanding babies.
Website: www.cry-sis.org.uk Helpline: +44 (0)8451 228 669
Every day 9 a.m. –10 p.m

NCT: National Childbirth Trust
Childbirth and parenting charity. Information on pregnancy, childbirth, breastfeeding, and parenthood.
Website: www.nct.org.uk
Support line: +44 (0)300 3300 700

Post-Adoption Centre

Offers advice and support with all aspects of adoption. Website: www.pac-uk.org

Email: advice@postadoptioncentre.org.uk

London office advice line: +44 (0) 20 7284 5879 Monday, Tuesday & Friday 10.00 a.m.–4.00 p.m. Wednesday & Thursday 2.00 p.m.–7.30 p.m

Leeds office advice line: +44 (0) 113 230 2100 Monday, Thursday & Friday 10.00 a.m.–1.00 p.m. Tuesday & Wednesday 4.00 p.m.–7.00 p.m.

Twins Trust

Provides information, a confidential helpline and mutual support networks for families of twins, triplets and more.

Website: www.twinstrust.org Email: enquiries@twinstrust.org.uk Tel: +44 (0) 1252 332 344

Index